Your Towns and Cities i

C000193248

Portsmouth
in the Great War

Sarah Quail

Pen & Sword
MILITARY

First published in Great Britain in 2014 by
PEN & SWORD MILITARY
an imprint of
Pen and Sword Books Ltd
47 Church Street
Barnsley
South Yorkshire S70 2AS

Copyright © Sarah Quail, 2014

ISBN 978 1 78346 276 6

The right of Sarah Quail to be identified as the author of
this work has been asserted by her in accordance with the Copyright,
Designs and Patents Act 1988.

A CIP record for this book is available from the British Library

All rights reserved. No part of this book may be reproduced or transmitted
in any form or by any means, electronic or mechanical including
photocopying, recording or by any information storage and retrieval
system, without permission from the Publisher in writing.

Printed and bound in England
by Page Bros, Norwich

Pen & Sword Books Ltd incorporates the imprints of
Pen & Sword Archaeology, Atlas, Aviation, Battleground, Discovery,
Family History, History, Maritime, Military, Naval, Politics, Railways,
Select, Social History, Transport, True Crime, and Claymore Press,
Frontline Books, Leo Cooper, Praetorian Press, Remember When,
Seaforth Publishing and Wharncliffe.

For a complete list of Pen and Sword titles please contact
Pen and Sword Books Limited
47 Church Street, Barnsley, South Yorkshire, S70 2AS, England
E-mail: enquiries@pen-and-sword.co.uk
Website: www.pen-and-sword.co.uk

Contents

This book is dedicated to
the people of Portsmouth, young and old,
men and women, who served this country at home
and abroad during the First World War.

Preface

I was very aware when I began work on this book that Portsmouth in the First World War was a well-explored subject already. Within a year of the end of hostilities one of the local newspapers, the *Evening News,* had published a memorial volume, *Portsmouth and the Great War.* It is not so much a history of the war as a chronicle of different sectors' war work. The book is illustrated with photographs by local photographer Stephen Cribb and also lists the names of the Portsmouth men who died in the conflict. It has been out of print for many years but the *Evening News's* successor title, *The News,* has reprinted it to mark the centenary of the First World War. More recently, Portsmouth writers such as John Sadden have published well-received books on the subject. The problem for me therefore was how best to strike out on my own and avoid too much repetition of previously-published sources?

I was fortunate. I had noticed material to do with the First World War in the Portsea Parish Magazines some years ago when I was working on a centenary history of the present church building, and when I looked at the bound volumes once again, it was clear that here was a rich – and unexplored – source of material. I was similarly lucky at the National Museum of the Royal Navy's Library in Portsmouth Naval Base. Looking at accession dates, it was clear that a lot of original material had been deposited by First World War veterans in the late twentieth century, possibly when their families were sorting out their effects. These are not official records. They are very personal, and I do not think that any of the writers I have quoted were writing for posterity. Their material ranges from a handful of letters to whole volumes, and often several of them, in which the writers record what they see and how they feel, their hopes and fears and, often, where they think the strategists have got it wrong! There are letters to mothers and fathers, to wives and girlfriends. Most of the diaries though seem to have been written for the sheer pleasure of putting pen to paper. This material constituted another unexplored source, this time on the experiences of naval men, the branch of the armed services whose story is inextricably entwined with that of the town of Portsmouth. This may not always have been their home town but it was often where they joined up, where their ship was based or where they trained over the years.

Other material has been drawn to my attention by friends and acquaintances who knew how keen I was to identify new sources. There may be criticism of my approach. The story I tell is not confined to domestic hearths but ranges round the world, and follows quite deliberately the main narrative of events during the First World War. It was Portsea curate, Ellis Edge-Partington, who said early in the war, 'Portsmouth can be found anywhere - Good Old Pompey!'

Acknowledgements

I am indebted to a number of individuals and institutions whose advice and assistance has enabled me to write this book. First of all, I must thank the National Museum of the Royal Navy (NMRN) for permission to quote material in the 'List of Books and Sources' at the back of this book and to reproduce photographs. I am also grateful to their library staff who courteously got out a great deal of material for me to study during the summer months of 2013. I am equally grateful to staff at the Portsmouth History Centre in the Central Library who gave me permission to quote material and in their turn produced a number of books and documents for me to look at, many of which had to be brought in from their out store. I must also acknowledge the fact that Lieutenant Rundell's letters are reproduced courtesy of Mr Jack Clayton, and the photographs of women dockyard workers by kind permission of the Portsmouth Royal Dockyard Historical Trust.

I must thank too the family of Dr Fred Gladstone for permission to quote from his diary, particularly his descendant, Deborah Aylward, and her husband, Meyrick, who first drew my attention to the doctor, his diary and his remarkable collection of photographs which they have most generously given me permission to reproduce. I am also grateful to several people at Portsmouth Grammar School who have helped me in different ways: Head of History, Simon Lemieux, the Headmaster's Personal Assistant, Jane Moody, and the School Archivist, John Sadden. John Sadden gave me access to the Percy F. Westerman Collection in the School Library. He also gave me permission to reproduce his own copy of a postcard of old boy, Lieutenant Norman

Holbrook VC, and answered many different questions with great patience. Simon Lemieux provided me with copies of the remarkable piece of work undertaken in 2000 by Third Year pupils, History Department staff and colleagues on 'OPs (Old Portmuthians) who died in the First World War', and I should express my gratitude here to the pupils, young men and women now in their late twenties, for their labours then.

Other people who have helped me with sources, answered my questions or given me assistance include Dave Jordan who generously lent me postcards of Portsmouth scenes to reproduce; Phil Parkinson of PLC Architects who lives and works today at 'Brankesmere', and generously lent me copies of pictures he took when he completed the restoration of this fine house; former colleague, Rosemary Phillips; Richard Brooks who gave me advice on Fred Jane and espionage matters; Nigel Gossop who is an invaluable source of information on Percy F. Westerman; former Royal Navy officer, Michael Dobson, who patiently answered questions on naval matters and Leigh Asher of *asherdesignandprint* who gave me invaluable assistance in preparing my illustrations for this book.

Finally, I must thank my husband who has lived patiently for the last twelve months with a project which proved a great deal more time-consuming and demanding than either of us anticipated when I began! Thank you!

Sarah Quail
June 2014

CHAPTER 1

Setting the Scene

Portsmouth in 1914 – Naval Port and Garrison Town –
Dreadnought Campaign

There were bodies, hundreds of them, in the water, and dead fish, and the surface of the sea was covered with oil as their ship crossed the battle area once again, scribbled Midshipman Arthur Layard in his diary. It was evening on Thursday, 1 June 1916. They had steamed south at great speed all the previous night on HMS *Indomitable,* trying to cut off the fleeing German fleet from their coast, and safety. Other writers recalled the same gruesome spectacle as they too crossed the battle area that day. The losses at Jutland were catastrophic for both sides, and particularly for the town of Portsmouth, the home of the Royal Navy, where six ships based there were sunk. Some 4,000 men, most of them living locally, were lost, and 1,500 families were left fatherless. Over the coming days, the Town Hall was besieged with anxious people wanting news of relatives and friends and, in many cases, help of one sort or another.

Following closely on these appalling losses, came the grim news of the sinking of another ship with strong local ties. This time it was HMS *Hampshire* which sank, after striking a German mine off Orkney some two hours after leaving Scapa Flow. The warship had Lord Kitchener and his staff on board, bound for Russia for talks. Only a handful of men survived. She was a Portsmouth ship and, yet again, there were many Portsmouth men on board. Losses on this scale at sea, and the wholesale destruction at the same time of local battalions of the Hampshire Regiment in the water-logged trenches of Flanders, had not been contemplated in the hot, heady days of early August 1914 when war was declared. It was not what was meant to happen. The Royal Navy was expected to meet and defeat the German fleet, probably in the North Sea, in an engagement reminiscent – and worthy – of Nelson's victory at the Battle of Trafalgar.

Earlier on that June morning, young Arthur Layard actually wrote that 'Beatty did a Nelson', and signalled 'the losses on both sides have been heavy but we hope to cut off and annihilate the whole German Fleet today. It is up to every man to do his utmost.' As for the British Army and its allies, they were expected to defeat the enemy in a major engagement in open countryside, like Wellington's victory at Waterloo one hundred years earlier when Napoleon was finally defeated. The First World War – the Great War – did not work out quite like this though.

Portsmouth still remembers this catastrophic conflict. Each year since the first Armistice Day on 11 November 1919, a moving ceremony has taken place in the former Town Hall (now Guildhall) Square, (the town was raised to the status of a city in 1926). It is led by local religious leaders in the presence of civic, naval and military dignitaries, and serving members of the armed forces. Nowadays, the ceremony takes place on Remembrance Sunday, the nearest Sunday to Armistice Day. Bare-headed and often in poor weather, Portsmouth marks the sacrifice of its men and women not only in two world wars but also on more recent battle fronts in a ceremony which has its origins almost a hundred years before in the aftermath of the First World War.

The Portsmouth Grammar School has particular reason to mark this occasion. Portsmouth's oldest school, founded in 1732 by Dr William Smith, garrison physician and local politician, is believed to have lost more old pupils in the two world wars than any other school of comparable size. As early as January 1915, local newspapers were reporting proudly that the school was a credit both to itself and to the town. In the space of three weeks before Christmas 1914, an astonishing number of former pupils had distinguished themselves: Lieutenant Holbrook had won the VC, Captain Langmaid the MC, Major French the DSO and Corporal Baker the DSM. The school had been beaten in the medals tables by only eleven other independent schools as regards old boys serving with the colours, and by only four other schools for the number of their young men 'mentioned in despatches'. The papers also pointed out that over half of Portsmouth Grammar School's Old Boys serving were in the Royal Navy who up to now had been given little opportunity to distinguish themselves. Given the chance, the tally of medals would have been even greater! Today, there are 127 names in gold letters on the Great War Memorial in the school library.

To better understand the role Portsmouth played in the First World War, it is important to have some understanding of what sort of town it was. First and foremost, it was a naval port and garrison town, and the home of the Royal Navy. It had grown significantly in recent years, on an island site on the South Coast measuring approximately 4 miles by 9 miles, separated from the Isle of Wight by the Solent. The first ship repair and victualing facilities were established here by Richard I in the late twelfth century. The town was conveniently situated at the mouth of a great natural harbour with a deep-water channel hugging

Portsmouth before the First World War summed up in a picture postcard.

the approaching shoreline and realised its potential in the early medieval period as a useful link in the King's line of communications with his lands in France. He gave the town its first royal charter in 1194. His brother, John, charged the Sheriff of Southampton in 1212 to put 'a good strong wall' round 'our dock at Portsmouth', and during the years that followed the town was a rendezvous for expeditionary forces as well as a developing trading centre. Henry VII designated the town a royal dockyard and garrison town, affirmation of its importance to the crown. War was the town's life blood and the sixteenth century antiquarian John Leland noted *c*.1540 that the town was 'bare and little occupied in time of pece[sic].' But with wars against the Dutch in the late seventeenth century, and the French for the best part of the eighteenth century, the dockyard became a major industrial enterprise, and the town spread rapidly beyond the confines of the original settlement at the harbour mouth.

This development gathered momentum during the nineteenth century with the extension of the dockyard in the 1840s, and between 1867 and 1881, when the area of the dockyard trebled in size – the Great Extension – from approximately 99 to 261 acres. The key feature of this latest development was three inter-connected basins with a combined area of 52 acres, with five docks and a range of adjacent

Men leaving Portsmouth Dockyard at Unicorn Gate. **(Jordan Collection).**

Launch of HMS **Dreadnought***, 10 February 1906.*

workshops. The threat of war with France had long gone. New tensions existed however towards the end of the century, between the United Kingdom and the newly-united German nation which was beginning to build a battle fleet of its own as part of a deliberate policy to challenge British naval supremacy. The conclusion of the *entente cordiale* between the United Kingdom and France in 1904 – loyally celebrated in Portsmouth – only exacerbated these tensions.

The dockyard work force more than doubled in size in thirty years, reflecting these political developments. It grew from 6,300 in 1881 to 7,976 in 1901, and from 10,439 in 1911, to 15,000 in 1914. Late Victorian and Edwardian shipbuilding was labour intensive. There was

Launch of HMS **King George V***, 9 October 1911.*

equipment for building ships in Portsmouth dockyard: sheer-legs, floating cranes, and the huge 240-ton capacity cantilever crane but ships were still, on the whole, constructed by manpower, and the more ships that were laid down, and the larger those ships, the more men were needed to build them.

Described by Portsmouth historian Ray Riley in *The Spirit of Portsmouth,* as 'the most tangible and jingoistic outcome of the race to produce ships capable of outgunning any other afloat' was HMS *Dreadnought*, 17,900 tons, launched by King Edward VII, in Portsmouth dockyard, on Saturday, 10 February 1906. At that time *Dreadnought* was the most powerful battleship in the world, and significantly larger than any of her predecessors. The ships' name in fact became synonymous with this entire class of ships. The predecessors were referred to as 'pre-dreadnoughts', and the later successors were called 'super-dreadnoughts'.

All records were beaten during construction. The keel was laid down on 2 October 1905, and the vessel was launched after being only five months on the stocks. HMS *Dreadnought* was commissioned on 3 October 1906, just one year after the first keel plates were laid. This pace was maintained by the dockyard workforce. It was Admiralty policy to build the first vessel in each of the dreadnought classes in a

Portsmouth Dockyard, 1916.

naval dockyard. Portsmouth dockyard workers had shown what they could do, and they were chosen to do the work. A new dreadnought went down the slipway almost every year after 1906, each larger and faster than the predecessor. The HMS *Bellerophon* in 1907 displaced 18,600 tons, and HMS *St Vincent* in 1908 displaced 19,250 tons. The latter was described at the launching by local newspaper editor W.G. Gates as greater in size than any ship which had gone down the slip before but this record was broken the following year, and in each successive year, as yet another ship was commissioned.

HMS *Neptune* was commissioned in 1909 displacing 19,900 tons, and HMS *Orion* (the first 'super-dreadnought'), in 1910 displacing 22,000 tons. The ship was described once again by Gates as 'the largest, fastest and heaviest warship ever set afloat at Portsmouth' but was overtaken by HMS *King George V* in 1911 displacing 23,400 tons. HMS *Iron Duke* was launched in 1912 displacing 25,000 tons and in the following year HMS *Queen Elizabeth* (the first oil-fuelled battleship) was launched displacing 27,500 tons.

The skilled men who built these ships and, in due course, the submarines which would play such a significant part in the coming conflict, lived within walking distance of the dockyard. Their houses stood in the decaying back streets of the original settlement of old

Town Hall and Queen Victoria Statue,   Portsmouth.

Town Hall Square, 1906, (Jordan Collection).

Commereial Road, Portsmouth.

Commercial Road and Town Hall Square looking north, c.1910.
(Jordan Collection).

Commercial Road, Post Office and Railway Station Entrance, c.1910.
(Jordan Collection).

Commercial Road,
Portsmouth.

Portsmouth, at the harbour mouth, in the adjacent eighteenth century suburb of Portsea, or in the new streets built beyond these confines and spreading now across Portsea Island. These were in the district of Landport, now the commercial and civic centre, where a new Town Hall was opened in 1890, and in the neighbourhoods of Buckland, Kingston and Milton. The streets were not particularly attractive. The oldest church on Portsea Island, St Mary's, Portsea, rebuilt in the 1880's, stood at the heart of these developments. The vicar, C.F. Garbett, later Archbishop of York, noted, '…the sheer ugliness which characterizes most of Portsmouth' in the Parish Magazine published in September 1918:

> 'The modern town has been built without a spark of imagination. Row after row of red brick boxes, with square or oblong holes in their walls, while here and there a street glazed with hideous white brick, but you may walk through miles of our streets without finding a house which has any mark of beauty. Oh, the drab dreariness and ugliness of our Portsmouth streets! And our public buildings, with the exception of the Town Hall, half a dozen churches, and one or two schools are no better. The buildings recently erected at public expense could not have been more unsightly if they had been the result of a competition for the 'most ugly' design. Here and there in old Portsmouth or Portsea you find some picturesque corner, and over the ramparts you have one really fine view of the entrance to the harbour, but elsewhere there is hardly anything to gratify or to develop the artistic instincts.'

Garbett was given to bouts of depression. His dyspeptic descriptions of his parish and its districts, and Portsmouth generally, do not take account of the leafier and, in parts, decidedly elegant, middle-class seaside suburb and naval outlier of Southsea.

Southsea developed concurrently with his parish along the southern shores of Portsea Island. This was where naval and army officers and their families, and most of Portsmouth's professional classes lived and worked, were schooled, shopped, went to church, exercised, promenaded and socialised. It is also where, once the railway arrived in Portsmouth in 1847, the middle classes came to enjoy the sea air and take a holiday. By 1885, more than half the properties in the Osborne

*Detail from O.S. 6 inch map of the seafront 1858,
revised 1932 showing barrack accommodation in
and adjoining the old town.*

South Parade Pier, Canoe Lake and adjacent beach from the air, c.1920. The size of the houses diminishes the further away you are from the sea.

Road and Clarence Parade areas of Southsea were lodging houses for seaside visitors and, as the century came to a close, the South Parade area and its adjacent streets, Florence Road, Beach Road and St Helen's Park Crescent developed similarly. Seaside hotels had opened too: the

'On the Parade, Southsea.' An image from the Illustrated London News, 19 August 1893.

Ladies Mile, Southsea, c.1905.

Queen's Hotel in 1861, the *Pier Hotel* in 1865, the *Beach Mansions Hotel* in 1866, the *Sandringham Hotel* in 1871, and the *Grosvenor Hotel* in 1880. There were also two piers by the time war broke out in 1914: Clarence Pier which had first opened in 1861 and South Parade

South Parade Pier, c.1905.

Southsea Beach and Promenade, c.1910. **(Jordan Collection).**

Pier which opened in 1879, but was badly damaged by fire in 1904. It was purchased subsequently by the town council who rebuilt it on a more ambitious scale and turned it into a most successful municipal undertaking.

Here, off the seafront, and in the vicinity of Palmerston Road and Osborne Road with their smart shops, Clarendon Road, Grove Road and Kent Road, was fashionable Southsea. St Jude's Church, a 'carriage' church, stood at the junction of Kent Road and Palmerston Road, and there was a large and well-attended Congregational Church,

Canoe Lake and area, c.1910. **(Jordan Collection).**

Elm Grove, Southsea, c.1910.

another 'carriage 'church, further down Kent Road at the top of Ashburton Road. The white *stucco* houses and terraces nearby, and the brick villas, most built in the last half of the nineteenth century, were the homes of the town's wealthier residents.

However despite these civilizing features, Portsmouth was still a heavily-defended naval port and garrison town. The first defences – a

King's Road, Southsea, c.1905.

Palmerston Road, Southsea, 1905. The decorations are to celebrate the 1904 **Entente Cordiale** *and the visit of the French (Navy) Northern Squadron in August 1905.*

wooden palisade on an earth embankment – had been put up round the town in the late fifteenth century when French raids had demonstrated how easy it was for an enemy to destroy town and dockyard and thus control shipping movements in the English Channel. The defences were improved and developed by each succeeding generation of military strategists culminating in the great ring of fortresses built round the greater Portsmouth area in the course of the nineteenth century. They were known locally as the 'Palmerston' forts as it was Lord Palmerston's government which in 1859 appointed the Royal Commission on the Defences of the United Kingdom which prompted their construction.

In the late eighteenth century, the first Southsea residents had in fact fled the constraints of living in a walled, garrison town with smoking chimneys, a poor water supply and inadequate waste disposal, and all the inconveniences of a night curfew. The walls on the landward side of old Portsmouth and Portsea were in fact demolished during the 1870s and 1880s, redundant now due to the dramatic improvements in

The Victoria Barracks, Royal Pier Hotel and Southsea Terrace viewed from Clarence Pier, c.1912.

the range and effectiveness of shore-based artillery, but in their place came new barrack accommodation not only for the large numbers of

A tramcar specially illuminated to mark the visit of the French Northern Squadron in August 1905.

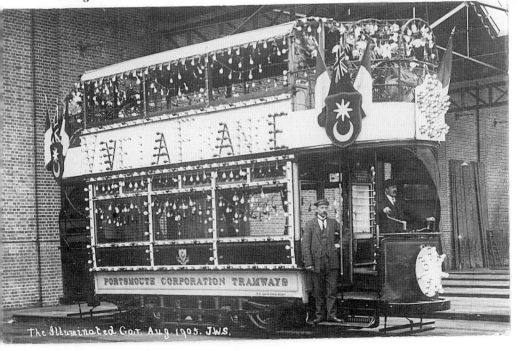

troops passing through the town on their way to far-flung corners of the British Empire, but for those men required to defend Portsmouth.

By 1914, there was an enormous military establishment occupying the barrack blocks in the north-east quarter of old Portsmouth – and occupied in part today by Portsmouth Grammar School. This was where Richard I built the King's House, his own quarters in the town, in the 1180s, and where Henry VIII had four great brewhouses built in the sixteenth century to supply his ships. In due course this site became barrack accommodation – Fourhouse Barracks. It was redeveloped several times during the nineteenth century into Cambridge and Clarence Barracks. Finally, in the 1880s, Clarence Barracks was enlarged and a new complex, Victoria Barracks, built on the recently demolished fortifications. Another large area of buildings was constructed by the Admiralty on the north side of Queen Street between 1899 and 1903 on land previously occupied by the Portsea defences. Until now seamen had been maintained on board ship in the harbour but it was now decided to bring them on shore and accommodate them in barracks – the naval barracks – like the army. Other large-scale barrack accommodation included the Royal Artillery Barracks at Hilsea built in 1854 and the Royal Marine Artillery Division's impressive and austere buildings at Eastney constructed in the 1860s.

Social facilities for servicemen over and beyond the ubiquitous public houses and sleazy lodging houses in parts of old Portsmouth and Portsea had been established in the town in the late nineteenth century. There was the Royal Sailors' Home in Queen Street, Portsea, established in 1851, the Soldiers' Institute, set up by Sarah Robinson in the now abandoned *Fountain Inn* in the High Street of old Portsmouth in 1874, and a Sailor's Rest opened by Agnes Weston in 1881. These establishments provided a wide range of much-needed facilities. There was clean and comfortable hostel accommodation, and dining rooms, baths, writing and reading rooms, rooms for concerts and film shows, and banking facilities and evening classes. The 'Aggie Weston' in fact became famous worldwide not only for its founder's concern for the moral welfare of seamen but for the welfare of their families too.

Portsmouth was in the Southern Military Command in 1914. Southern Command's headquarters were just outside Salisbury. The

Portsmouth Garrison's commander – the General Officer Commanding – was Major General W.E. Blewitt, and the town was the headquarters of the 9th Infantry Brigade and the Southern Coast Defences, within which were a considerable number of troops. In fact there were over 6,000 men recorded in barracks in the 1911 census. The 9th Infantry Brigade itself had four infantry battalions in different barracks in the area; the Victoria and Cambridge Barracks in Portsmouth, across the harbour in Gosport and at Parkhurst on the Isle of Wight. The brigade would be part of the British Expeditionary Force sent to France in August when war was declared.

There were a number of artillery units in the town responsible for its defences. The 140th and 141st Batteries of the Royal Artillery were at Hilsea Barracks and, based at Clarence Barracks, were No.37 Company and No.42 Company of the Royal Garrison Artillery, part of the area's inner defences, and No.29 Company and No.67 Company, part of the outer defences. The Army Service Corps, concerned with vital issues of supplies, transport and accommodation was based at the Colewort Barracks on St George's Road which became in due course the site for a power station and is occupied today by housing. The Royal Army Medical Corps was at garrison headquarters in the High Street and in the new Alexandra Military Hospital at Cosham. The Royal Engineers were at Milldam Barracks and the Army Ordnance Department was on HM Gunwharf (Gunwharf Quays).

There was also a large Territorial Force in Portsmouth whose duties were to defend the town and immediate area in the event of war. The lists of their honorary officers are a roll call of the town's business and professional interests: men such as Lieutenant Colonel Cheke; architect, Major Cogswell; printer and stationer, Captain Barrell; artist and Royal Academician, Captain W.H. Wyllie; Captain Bevis, Lieutenant King and Second Lieutenants Couzens and Sherwin, respectively a builder, a land agent and a solicitor. With their fellow territorials, they and their families would continue to serve Portsmouth's interests long after the end of the war. The Portsmouth Troop of the Hampshire Carabiniers Yeomanry (A Squadron) met at the Drill Hall, Governors Green as did the Hampshire Royal Garrison Artillery (TF) and the Wessex Division Royal Army Medical Corps, 3rd Wessex Field Ambulance. The headquarters of the 1st and 2nd

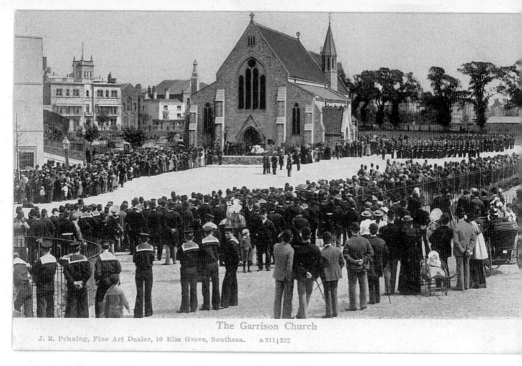

The Garrison Church

J. R. Pelning, Fine Art Dealer, 10 Elm Grove, Southsea.   a 211|222

Church Parade, Garrison Church, Governor's Green, c.1910.

Hants Batteries and Ammunition Column of the 1st Wessex Brigade Royal Field Artillery was in St Paul's Road. Other territorial forces included the Hampshire (Fortress) Royal Engineers whose headquarters was in Hampshire Terrace, the 6th Battalion Hampshire Regiment (A, B, C, D, E, F, G and H companies) whose headquarters was the Connaught Drill Hall in Stanhope Road and the 9th Battalion Hampshire Regiment (Cyclists) whose base was also in the Connaught Drill Hall.

Major General Blewitt and his family lived at Government House, a large red-brick mansion, standing in its own grounds, in Cambridge Road. Government House was built in 1882 on land released by the demolition of the fortifications. Old Government House in the High Street was now part of the local military headquarters. This house had replaced the ancient and very dilapidated Governor's accommodation on Grand Parade in 1826. Only the chapel, the Garrison Church, survives, much restored, today. Charles II had married his Portuguese bride, Catherine of Braganza, in this house in 1662, and it was here that the Allied Sovereigns, the Prince Regent, the King of Prussia and the Emperor of Russia had met in 1814 to celebrate what they believed was the end of hostilities against Napoleonic France.

Section of O.S. 1:500 map showing Military Headquarters, High Street, 1870.

The Garrison Commander's post can be traced back to at least the late thirteenth century when the first name can be identified of a Constable of Portchester Castle who was also governor of the towns of 'Portchestre, Portesmouthe and of the Country about'. This title survived until the reign of Henry VIII when Portsmouth acquired its own captain or governor, reflecting the growing military importance of the town and its defences. The governorship was actually abolished in 1834, but the duties were undertaken thereafter by the Lieutenant Governor and, later, when that post was deleted, by the General Officer Commanding.

The flagship of the commander-in-chief was Nelson's flagship, HMS *Victory,* still afloat in Portsmouth Harbour, although the general work of the flagship was carried out in the Royal Naval Barracks at the top of Queen Street. The commander-in-chief in 1914 was Admiral of the Fleet The Hon. Sir Hedworth Meux who, as Captain The Honourable Hedworth Lambton (he was a younger son of the Earl of

HMS **Victory**, *Nelson's*
flagship, and the
flagship of the
Commander-in-Chief,
Portsmouth, c.1910.

Durham) and commander of one of the largest warships of the time, HMS *Powerful,* had gained fame in 1899 for leading the Naval Brigade to relieve the beleaguered British forces at the Siege of Ladysmith. The nation was enchanted with the exploits of the Naval Brigade, and Captain Lambton became a well-known public figure.

When HMS *Powerful* returned to Portsmouth harbour, the ship was greeted with thunderous applause from vessels moored alongside or at anchor, all dressed overall with flags; their crews swarming along the yards and cheering themselves hoarse. On the jetty more crowds of men, women and children waved hats and handkerchiefs and roared their delight at the sight of the returning heroes. A succession of distinguished appointments followed for Lambton in which he saw service on the King's yacht, *Victoria and Albert,* followed in the next few years by service in the Channel Fleet, in the Mediterranean and on the China Station. He made an advantageous marriage to the widow of Henry Cadogan, Viscount Chelsea, in 1910 and shortly afterwards inherited a substantial fortune from the childless Valerie, Lady Meux, reputedly a former actress and the widow of brewer Sir Henry Brent Meux, on the condition that he change his name to Meux. He was appointed to be Commander-in-Chief, Portsmouth in 1912 and lived at Admiralty House in the dockyard. The dockyard had a dedicated team of officers, led by an Admiral Superintendent and his deputy who was also Captain of the Dockyard and King's Harbour Master.

With over 25 percent of the town's male working population in uniform (over 23,000), local people were used to seeing service men on the streets. They were marched regularly through the town, often to and from the railway station and their barrack accommodation. There were exercises on Southsea Common and military parades and march-pasts, on barrack parade grounds as well as on Sunday mornings outside the Garrison Church and inside the Naval Barracks. Naval and military outfitters, and suppliers of all descriptions still occupied premises on the main thoroughfares: High Street in old Portsmouth, Queen Street and The Hard in Portsea and, to a limited extent, King's Road and Palmerston Road in Southsea. Public houses were located on almost every street corner, particularly in the less affluent parts of the town. Altogether, there were almost 600 on Portsea Island alone in 1914, owned mainly by brewers Brickwoods, Portsmouth United Breweries and Longs.

There was also a wide range of live entertainment – drama, opera, ballet, music hall and variety – available in a number of local venues. There was the New Theatre Royal which opened in 1884 and was given a major refit in 1900 by the foremost theatrical architect and designer of the day, Frank Matcham. Two more large theatres followed in 1907: the *Hippodrome*, almost opposite the *New Theatre Royal* in what once was Commercial Road, and the *King's Theatre* in Albert Road,

Southsea, designed again by Matcham. The *Prince's Theatre* in Lake Road, another Matcham design, was also renovated at this time. Moving-picture shows were a very popular source of entertainment too. They caught on quickly in Portsmouth and by 1915 there were almost thirty different licensed moving picture halls with a capacity of 17,752 seats. They included local theatres, armed services premises, public halls and even local hospitals as well as premises newly-built or adapted specifically for showing moving pictures (cinemas).

There were large numbers of seafarers among local families. Traditionally, Portsmouth was a seafaring community. If a boy did not go into the dockyard or join the family trade or business when he left school before 1914 he went usually into the Royal Navy or, occasionally, the army. It is not possible to calculate how many of the 20,000 men listed in the 1911 Census as 'Navy and Marines (Ashore and in Port)' were actually Portsmouth men, but in the event of a naval disaster, losses were devastating and whole neighbourhoods descended into mourning. The worst loss before 1914 was the unnecessary sinking of HMS *Victoria* off Tripoli in 1893. Almost half the crew of over 700 men were lost, many of them Portsmouth men. A national appeal, championed by Agnes Weston, raised £50,000 in three weeks, the equivalent of £5,000,000 today, to help the dependents of those who lost their lives.

The Mayor of Portsmouth actually set up a Naval Disasters Fund in 1908 in response to the loss in April that year of two Royal Navy ships in the Solent with local men on board: HMS *Tiger* and HMS *Gladiator.* Built in 1900, *Tiger* was a 380-ton destroyer and was taking part in a Home Fleet exercise on 2 April some twenty miles south of the Isle of Wight to test defences against torpedo boats. The ship crossed the bow of an adjacent cruiser, HMS *Berwick,* and was sliced in half. The bow section of *Tiger* sank almost immediately, but the stern section stayed afloat long enough for most of the crew to be rescued. Sadly, the captain and twenty-seven of the crew were lost. Later in the month, on 25 April, HMS *Gladiator,* a 12-year-old twin-screw 5,750-ton cruiser with a crew of 250 men, was hit by the American liner SS *St Paul,* 11,629-ton displacement, off Yarmouth in a blinding snowstorm. Miraculously only one officer and 28 men died. Over £10,000 was raised for the local Disasters Fund. The mayor also raised funds for the families of local men lost when HMS *Bedford* sank in the Straits of

Korea in 1910, and another remarkable sum of over £6,000 for the families of men lost on Portsmouth-based submarines A3 and B2 in 1912.

There were also large numbers of women who worked in Portsmouth in the early twentieth century. Seamen's widows, and the wives and unmarried daughters of men either away at sea or, if they were soldiers, posted abroad, made up a large available female labour force. They had played a significant role in the economic life of the town throughout the nineteenth century. With the wives of dockyard workers, these women worked as dressmakers, seamstresses and stay makers, and accounted for between 21 and 33 percent of the town's industrial employment between 1841 and 1901. Sailors' widows had even worked in the dockyard making flags, overalls and work bags, and in the ropehouses on winding machines. In 1911, almost 8,000 of them still constituted approximately 33 percent of the female workforce of 26,000, and 10 percent of the combined male and female workforce of 102,000 in the town.

As for local politics, with an electorate made up largely of naval, military and dockyard interests, the Conservative Party, associated with rearmament and dockyard employment, was on the whole the dominant force in the town at both municipal and parliamentary levels both before and after the war, and indeed for much of the twentieth century. Two Liberals MPs were returned to Westminster in the Liberal 'landslide' of 1906, but in the two parliamentary elections of 1910 there was a swing back to the Conservatives when popular naval champion and hero, Admiral Lord Charles Beresford, and Bertram Falle, a barrister, were returned in both contests.

Cautious progress was the hallmark of municipal endeavour during these years. A Municipal College of Science, Arts, Technology, Commerce and Pure & Applied Arts opened in 1908. Agreement was also reached that year to open a women's teacher training college to supply the town's teaching needs and several slum clearance schemes were underway at long last in Portsea. It was not enough though for Cyril Garbett, the vicar of Portsea, who railed regularly against the failings, as he saw them, of the council in his letters to parishioners in the parish magazines. Housing was a particular issue for him and by the end of the war, the only answer for him was a new council:

'The truth of the matter is a new Town Council is required. Among its members there are of course some who are active and vigorous, and to whose enterprise and energy the town owes a debt of gratitude. But I am putting the matter quite bluntly, the Council as a whole is weak and apathetic; a number of its members have no real knowledge of either the responsibilities or possibilities of local government; they really owe their places to a party caucus and the general apathy of the electorate. Before the next election good citizens who are tired of the party methods of selection ought to meet together and decide to run independent candidates, men and women. But if this is to be done, some of our best citizens must be prepared to set aside their disinclination for the atmosphere of the Council chamber, and accept nomination as a matter of public duty.'

Portsmouth's 'best citizens' might have been forgiven however for feeling disinclined in 1918 to answer the vicar's call to do their public duty. Many of them must have felt that by then they had given their all.

CHAPTER 2

Eager for the Fight

*War declared – Wyllie Family – War footing – Aliens – Spies –
Naval Reservists called out – Recruiting Campaign – Portsmouth
Battalions – Distress Committee – Licensing Restrictions –
Volunteer Training Corps – War Work in Milton – First casualties
– Heligoland Bight – Coronel – Falkland Islands – Miss
Gwendoline Kyffin*

War was declared late at night on 4 August 1914. Marion Wyllie, the
wife of artist and Royal Academician, and local territorial officer W.H.
Wyllie, recorded the moment in her autobiography, *We Were One.* The
family was living in Tower House, near the Round Tower, on Point, in
the old town. The house was in a spectacular position, overlooking the
harbour entrance. Bill – as he was called by Marion – had a studio on
the first floor with a huge north-facing window looking up the harbour.
In those days Point was a crowded, lively area of the old town which
suited the faintly Bohemian Wyllie family famously. Marion Wyllie
recalled the occasion vividly:

> 'As I came… into the dining-room I saw our second son, Billie, at
> the window. "Take it down, Mater," he said, "I am reading." And I
> took down the declaration of war that was being flashed from Block
> House across the water to England at large, at a quarter to twelve
> midnight.
>
> 'Billie was waiting for the car to fetch him to join his regiment,
> the 3rd Durhams. It came all too soon. We said good-bye, and he,

Tower House today from the top of the Round Tower.

too, woke the quiet echoes down the silent alley. As I turned round to go back into the house, I looked up and saw the sentry at the top of the old Round Tower that abuts on our terrace silhouetted against the big, round harvest moon.'

The following day, August Bank Holiday, she reported:

'…the trippers came in their hundreds down our normally quiet little street. Footsteps! Footsteps!! Footsteps!!! – all day long – that reminded me of Dickens's 'Tale of Two Cities', and the footsteps that Lucie Manette was always hearing.

' Our fourth son, Bob, went out to them as the trippers crushed through the doors on to our terrace, and asked what they wanted to see.

'"Why," was the answer, "to see the boom run across the harbour." But nothing happened that day.'

Billie and Bob would both be killed in the war.

The Official Declaration was issued by the Foreign Office at 12.15am on 5 August 1914. It was a Wednesday:

'Owing to the summary rejection by the German Government of the request made by His Majesty's Government for the assurance that the neutrality of Belgium would be respected, His Majesty's Ambassador in Berlin has received his passports, and His Majesty's

Town Hall, Portsmouth, c.1910.

TOWN HALL, SOUTHSEA

Government has declared to the German Government that a state of war exists between Great Britain and Germany as from 11pm on August 4th.'

As news spread in the town that night of the British ultimatum to Germany, the tension amongst the crowds which gathered in the Town Hall Square was palpable, said the *Portsmouth Times,* exacerbated by the fact that the light illuminating the Town Hall clock was extinguished as they waited, and as the ultimatum expired. The paper was consoled however by the fact that the direction of the war had been entrusted to two 'capable, proved and tried administrators', Admiral Sir John Jellicoe, whose father lived in Ryde, it informed its readers, comfortingly, and Lord Kitchener. Jellicoe was an experienced naval officer who had supported the dreadnought building programme and was put in command of the Grand Fleet on the outbreak of war. Lord Kitchener was the hero of Omdurman, a field marshal and colonial administrator who was appointed Secretary of State for War at the beginning of the conflict.

Portsmouth moved rapidly onto a war footing. Strict regulation of shipping movements was introduced at once in the Inner Defence Area by order of the commander-in-chief. Movement was forbidden at night or in fog, and rules were laid down for the movement of vessels within this area during daylight hours. No vessel was allowed to enter port without being examined by an officer off the west end of the Isle of Wight. The Needles passage was closed. No vessel was allowed in without a pilot, and none allowed out without permission, and no one was allowed to approach a warship or naval establishment without authority. The regulations also indicated that a boom would be put in place across the harbour entrance, as the Wyllie family discovered. The authorities were very much aware that the German military and naval hierarchies were all too familiar with the configuration of Portsmouth dockyard, the town and its environs. As recently as 1907, the German Emperor had arrived in Portsmouth on the Royal Yacht *Hohenzollern* with a squadron of German warships, and been received with all the honours due him by local civic and armed service leaders.

The garrison was strengthened, and black-out regulations were introduced to protect the town from airship attack. Every second street lamp was put out, and those left burning were deeply shaded. Blinds in private houses had to be lowered or curtains pulled half an hour after sunset, and tradesmen had to ensure that no light from their premises could be discerned. All bells, including the Town Hall 'Pompey' Chimes, were silenced, and the seafront, and the beaches, screened off with barbed wire defences. A roundup of foreign nationals, aliens as they were called then, began a few days after the outbreak of war too, amid feverish debate about the possibility of German spies embedded in the town. Only the year before Portsea dentist, William Clare, had been caught with documents in his possession on the development of torpedoes at HMS *Vernon* for which Germany had offered him £300. He was sentenced to five years penal servitude.

Most foreign nationals had in fact been identified within the last four years. The Chief Constable was empowered now to issue warrants to detain and search the premises of anyone suspicious. If the suspicions were well-founded the detainee was handed over to the Special Branch. Several alleged spies were in fact arrested including a girl in Pelham Road, Southsea. This was probably the young woman about whom Fred T. Jane, the naval analyst and sometime intelligence officer of *Fighting Ships* fame, who lived in Southsea, expressed regret. 'Some time back', he wrote, 'an Army officer and I sent an awful pretty girl to limbo. Having done it we asked each other – Don't you feel an awful swine?' The actual number of foreign nationals – or aliens as they were called then – registered in the county of Hampshire at the outbreak of war was 1,600. Most were German but they included many other nationalities living in the prohibited area which included of course Portsmouth. Germans and Austrians had to obtain permits to remain in the area. They were often subject to harassment which usually meant they got their windows smashed.

By early 1915, following the initial round-up, there were 4,000 men and women interned on prison ships in Portsmouth Harbour. This was reminiscent of the treatment of French and American prisoners of war in the late eighteenth and early nineteenth centuries, and there was an outcry locally. The protestors were concerned not so much about the welfare of the internees but by the security risk. These people were in custody in the middle of Portsmouth dockyard which was itself at the heart of the Inner Defence Area. Surely this was imperilling the nation's security? In an answer to a question in the House of Commons from local MP, Lord Charles Beresford, the First Lord of the Admiralty, Winston Churchill, admitted that the situation was not ideal but that they were doing their best to find alternative accommodation. He was as good as his word. Within two weeks, the local papers were able to report that prison ships had gone from the harbour and those at Motherbank would be emptied soon and their occupants sent to camps.

There are tantalizing glimpses of putative spies across a range of narratives throughout the war. Lieutenant James Colvill was in the West Indies in November 1913 on HMS *Lancaster* and noted in his diary, now in the National Museum of the Royal Navy (NMRN) Library in Portsmouth Naval Base, that both he and a fellow officer on another ship had received letters from an unknown, so-called 'young lady,' Dorothy Chalmers, living in Southport, who was looking for a 'correspondence friend.' Fortunately, he recalled a recent memorandum warning that people ashore might be trying to find out about the service, and any such letters should be shown to the captain. At Scapa Flow in April 1915, he recorded another spy incident. One of the seamen had been arrested for being a German agent. A letter was apprehended in which the seaman apologized for not being able 'to do what he was here for.' It was addressed to a foreign barber in London.

There is another oblique reference to a spy in Able Seaman Sydney Bland's diary, also in the NMRN Library. He was on HMS *Vengeance* in late June 1915. The ship had put in to Malta on its way home to England to pay off after time spent patrolling the entrance to the Dardanelles and landing troops on the Gallipoli peninsula. Before they left Malta they 'took on board a lady spy.' In another incident during June 1916, a German, described as an 'eye specialist', was given three months hard labour by Marylebone Police Court in London. He was charged with failing to register as an enemy alien. In the course of a lecture tour he had visited Portsmouth, among other places, registering himself as a British subject. There was another local case in the same year to do with an individual who was prosecuted for sketching a battleship. He was convicted but the Bench was persuaded by his defence that it was a temporary aberration. He had been employed by a Portsmouth dairy for many years.

However, as late as July 1918 Mr Thomas Davies, Portsmouth's Chief Constable, felt it necessary to issue an official notice entitled

'Beware of Spies'. The public were told in no uncertain terms not to talk about what they were doing or going to do; not to discuss naval or military affairs, or ship movements, with strangers or foreigners; not to trust anyone they did not know; to report anyone who tried to inveigle them into divulging information and warning that want of care might help the enemy and imperil lives.

That England was on the verge of war in early August 1914 had certainly been clear for some weeks in Portsmouth. The previous month, there had been a special mobilization of the Fleet, ostensibly to test the efficiency of the reserve system. However, in reality, it was because, in the words of Gates, in *Records of the Corporation,* the Admiralty 'foresaw the early use of the fleet in terrible earnest.' Gates recorded that the naval spectacle was unprecedented in naval history and outdid any previous fleet review which had taken place at Spithead. There were 24 Dreadnoughts; 35 pre-Dreadnoughts; 18 armoured cruisers; 31 protected and light cruisers; 78 destroyers and a number of seaplanes.

Altogether, there were 40 miles of ships drawn up in twelve long lines. Manoeuvres began on 16 July 1914 and finished on 20 July when the entire 'armada' put to sea and passed in a single line in front of the King's yacht which was anchored off the Nab Tower. The Wyllie family had watched events that day from their tower:

> '...with eyes glued to the telescopes. First came the super-Dreadnoughts and Dreadnoughts, then the Agamemnons, then the

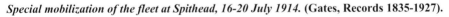

Special mobilization of the fleet at Spithead, 16-20 July 1914. (Gates, Records 1835-1927).

great battle cruisers, and one after another, as they passed His Majesty, the bands played a part of the march from 'Norma'. In time, the leading ship had sunk below the horizon, leaving only a great cloud of smoke that slowly spread into a haze, seeming to stretch into infinity.'

More evidence that the country was moving onto a war footing came shortly afterwards, a week before war was actually declared, on Wednesday, 29 July, with the sudden recall of all soldiers, sailors and marines. The following day armed guards appeared on the seafront and outside government property, as Marion Wyllie observed. When darkness fell, searchlights, installed on the front, began sweeping the Solent, Spithead and the night skies, to the delight of crowds who came to see the spectacle.

The Bank Holiday on 6 August, two days after war was declared, was curious, the *Portsmouth Times* reported the following day in its first roundup of local war news. There were no excursions to the Isle of Wight and there were no off-duty troops or seamen on the streets. However, Royal Naval Reserve (RNR) men had begun pouring into town in response to the call out on 4 August. They were 'in silk hat and frock coats', 'fishermen's garb' and 'the dress in which they had been following the plough', according to Gates in another publication, *Portsmouth and the Great War.* They marched to the Naval Barracks to the cheers of crowds on the pavements and within a week every ship was fully-manned and, said Gates, the naval establishments ashore were overflowing with men ready to go to sea once again. However, as a gesture that night to the expectations of the Bank Holiday crowds, military bands played selections of music on the parade ground in Victoria Barracks, and the public were admitted to listen.

For three months it was not necessary to recruit men for the navy so their recruiting officer, Lieutenant Commander William Barrett, turned his hand to recruiting men for the army. Photographs show two small tents he put up in the Town Hall Square, one flying the White Ensign and the other, the Union Jack and there, he and his team signed up a steady stream of volunteers. By the time the voluntary system of enlistment was replaced by compulsory military service for unmarried men between the ages of 18 and 41 in January 1916, Barrett had enlisted thousands of recruits.

The Territorials stepped up now to do their duty defending the town. The Hampshire (Fortress) Royal Engineers (RE) were mobilized at the beginning of the week. On the day war was declared, the 4th Battalion and 6th Battalion (Duke of Connaught's Own) Hampshire Regiment 'responded to the call'. The 4th arrived from Winchester in the morning. The 6th Hampshire, Portsmouth's home battalion, had been in camp on Salisbury Plain for a week. They were recalled to headquarters at the Connaught Drill Hall where they arrived on Monday and were greeted enthusiastically at the town station. They were at full strength with 730 officers and men. The 1st Wessex Brigade of the Royal Field Artillery (RFA) also mobilized. The Hants Carabiniers and local companies of the Royal Army Medical Corps also proceeded to their allotted stations.

Further, it was reported in the local papers that large numbers of horses were being commandeered in the town for military use, and that equally large numbers of men had rushed to the army and navy recruiting depots. An anti-war meeting took place in the Town Hall Square on the night war was declared but it was shouted down and the speaker was attacked. This was not the time or the place for such sentiments. Portsmouth was a town which knew all about the need to keep this country's sea lanes open, and protect our colonial empire overseas in Asia and Africa. After all, this was where HMS *Dreadnought* was built. Portsmouth was ready – and eager - for the fight. In a florid passage in *Portsmouth and the Great War*, Gates expressed the view that never before had there been, '...such perfect unity, such community of thought and sentiment, as in the opening days of the war. All political clamours ceased, all class distinctions were swept away, the Call for Service vibrated in every breast.'

Men and, in due course, munitions and money would be the local war cries, as they were nationally. Portsmouth newspapers gave instructions on 'How to join the Army,' and where to find the recruiting office which at this stage was at 19 Commercial Road. Gates quotes the first appeal by the War Office for men to join the Colours. It was published the day after war was declared: 'YOUR KING AND COUNTRY NEEDS YOU Will you answer your country's call? Each day is fraught with the gravest possibilities, and at this very moment the Empire is on the brink of the greatest War in the history of the world. In this crisis your country calls on her young unmarried men to rally round the flag and enlist in the ranks of her Army. If every patriotic young man answers her call, England and her Empire will emerge stronger and more united than ever. If you are unmarried and between 18 and 30 years old, will you answer your country's call? JOIN THE ARMY TODAY'

It was an irresistible invitation. The Recruiting Office was overwhelmed, and long queues formed outside. Local men enlisted, and were deployed to ships and regiments, the length and breadth of the British Isles. They would serve in every theatre of war. This is clear in research undertaken by third-year pupils and their teachers in the history department at Portsmouth Grammar School into old boys who died in the First World War. The men who died served in over thirty different regiments and at least twelve ships, as well as the Royal Marine Light Infantry, Royal Marine Artillery, and the Royal Flying Corps. Insofar as the sources permitted, it was possible to track something of each man's family history, school and service career, and details of his death. They included local brewer Sir John Brickwood's eldest son, Arthur; Sir Arthur Conan Doyle's youngest brother, Innes; the sons of many of Portsmouth's leading business and professional families as well as scholarship boys and the boys of families in seriously reduced circumstances. However, these men's stories are part of their regiments' histories, the school's history and, it can be argued, the histories of other towns, cities and regions. More relevant to Portsmouth is the story of the Hampshire Regiment and its battalions of regular, professional soldiers, many of whom came from Portsmouth; and the three battalions of local, mainly Portsmouth, men who were recruited now and over the coming months into three volunteer battalions of the Hampshire Regiment, in response to Lord Kitchener's call to arms. It is their story which is traced in these pages.

The fact that more than half of those who had crossed to France in early August were now casualties, and that one in ten had been killed, seems to have done little to dim the enthusiasm of local recruits. Lord Kitchener's appeal for his Second Army and 100,000 men was embraced locally. Lord Kitchener had asked that the machinery of the political parties could be placed at his disposal to take the recruiting programme forward. This was agreed nationally and, locally, Unionists, Liberals and Labour followed suit.

On 20 August, a small meeting was convened in the town hall by the mayor, Councillor J.H. Corke, with the local MPs and the military, to consider how best to respond to the request. A recruiting committee – the Parliamentary Recruiting Committee - was appointed to develop a scheme 'for the encouragement of a speedy response to the appeal for men'. The committee would arrange public meetings and find appropriate speakers. In addition, until the setting up of local tribunals following the introduction of compulsory military service, it would be the sole body, called the Advisory Committee from December 1915, assisting the local recruiting officer with claims for exemption.

For the moment though, a telegram was sent to the Secretary of State for War on 1 September 1914 offering to raise a battalion, and an acknowledgement was received welcoming the proposal. The campaign was launched at a densely-packed meeting in the town hall two days later. So great was the crowd of people trying to get into the building that an overflow meeting took place on the steps of the town hall. Sir Bertram Falle, one of the town's MPs, left the main meeting to address this gathering. Inside the hall, Lord Charles Beresford, Sir Bertram's fellow-MP for Portsmouth, rallied the meeting with a stirring speech after which it was moved that they:

> '…being fully convinced that the Government used its utmost efforts to maintain the peace of Europe, that in honour it was compelled to observe its Treaty for the maintenance of the integrity of the Kingdom of Belgium, and its friendly arrangements and understanding with France, enthusiastically approves of the action it has taken in connection with the War, and pledges itself to use its utmost efforts to assist in raising more recruits, so necessary at this crisis, to resist the aggressive action of Germany.'

The first recruits were signed up for the new Portsmouth Battalion at the end of the meeting, and for days afterwards men lined up outside the recruiting offices to enlist. As agreed, the campaign was managed by the staff of the local political parties. Men enlisted for three years or for as long as the war lasted. The battalion would be attached to the Hampshire Regiment and, to distinguish these new battalions from the battalions of regular men, they were known, at least in the early years of the war, as service battalions. Training began at once. The new recruits were drilled on Southsea Common. They were a motley crew in the early days. They had no uniform and no arms. The factories just could not turn out sufficient equipment to meet demand nationally. The War Office asked the mayor to devise some sort of interim uniform locally. Khaki cloth was not obtainable but a blue cloth was found which was used until proper uniforms could be obtained.

There was no spare barrack accommodation either in which to house the new battalion so they lived at home, and were each paid a guinea (21 shillings) per week to cover their bed and board. Those who did not live locally were put up in the Sailors' Rest and other similar establishments. Recruiting for this first battalion was completed by the spring and on 15 April 1915 Portsmouth's Own Battalion paraded on Southsea Common, watched by a large and tearful gathering of families, friends and the general public. They marched away to the station, led by Colonel C.E.R. Isherwood, to complete their training elsewhere. They were accompanied on their way by the lively and, with

The First Portsmouth, the 14th (Service) Battalion of the Hampshire Regiment marches away to complete training on 15 April 1915. **(Gates, Records 1835-1927.)**

the benefit of hindsight, poignant tunes of their own band playing 'Fall in and Follow Me!', 'I wonder if you'll miss me sometimes?' and 'Tipperary'. The instruments were provided by public subscription.

Recruiting for a second battalion began straight away not only in the town itself but in surrounding districts. The Parliamentary Recruiting Committee supplied an armoured car for the campaign which was ably assisted by the efforts of several well-known performers then appearing in local theatres. They included French actress Mademoiselle Gaby Deslys and comedian Harry Lauder. Whether it was their help, outrage at the bombardment of West Hartlepool or news of Belgian atrocities, and the sinking of the RMS *Lusitania*, this battalion was raised even more quickly than the first which is remarkable given that 17,000 men were now working in the dockyard. The last of the 1,100 recruits was signed up on 10 September, and the battalion marched away on 20 October to Witley to complete training. They were led by Major H.P.C. O'Farrell, and strode along to the music of their own band; again the instruments were a gift from local townsfolk. On this occasion, they had been drawn up in the Town Hall Square to be inspected by the mayor before they marched to the station and it was with considerable difficulty that they made their way through the cheering crowds to the trains.

Lists opened for a third battalion on 11 September, the day after the completion of the second battalion. A recruiting rally took place on Southsea Common on 2 October which was a great boost and by the end of the year the third battalion was complete and left for Winchester on 3 January 1916 where the men served as a reserve for the other two battalions. It was a remarkable achievement. Within fifteen months Portsmouth raised three battalions each of 1,100 men. The Mayor, Councillor Corke, was honoured with a knighthood for his and his recruiting team's efforts.

Councillor Corke was also instrumental in setting up the Portsmouth Distress Committee in late August 1914. This committee was established to deal with cases of distress which were likely to arise in consequence of war, such as unemployment, loss of earnings and damage, loss or injury through air raids. The Prince of Wales' National Relief Fund, to give it its correct title, was administered for these purposes through County Relief Committees and District Relief Sub

Committees. Portsmouth, as a county borough, set up its own Relief Committee under the auspices initially of the local Soldiers' and Sailors' Families' Association.

When war had broken out this was the only machinery available to deal with issues arising to do with service men and their families, and the local organizer, social worker Miss E.H. Kelly, and her volunteer team of ladies, moved quickly to install the organization in rooms in the Town Hall. As their funding came through the National Relief Fund (it was raised locally but managed and distributed nationally), it was known as the National Relief Sub-Committee but carried on under the rules of the Soldiers' and Sailors' Families' Association until late 1916 when it became the War Pensions Committee. An initial appeal for funds elicited over £2,000 from the town's leading citizens, and by the end of the year over £14,000 had been raised locally for the fund. The *Portsmouth Times* advised its readers that it was worth subscribing to this fund as a disproportionate number of the local population was likely to join up or be affected by the war compared with other towns, and would therefore be deserving of assistance. The paper also reported that Portsmouth would gain more from these arrangements than it was likely to pay in.

In fact the need soon became clear. Two sub-committees were set up, one to deal with armed service applications for relief and another to deal with civilian cases. At a meeting of the Civilian Sub-Committee, held in the town hall on 20 August, the same day in fact as the meeting held by the mayor to launch the recruitment drive for a Second Army, Sir John Brickwood announced that he had taken on thirty-two girls to replace men who had joined up. It was the first time he had employed female labour, and he was pleased to do so because the women needed work. The outbreak of war had been devastating for local tailoresses, milliners and staymakers. He reported that in many of the corset factories half-time was being worked, and pieceworkers faced poor prospects because the public were just not buying.

The women had in fact been paid well below the minimum wage laid down by the Trade Board Act before the outbreak of war anyway, and local suffrage groups and other sympathizers had come together to consider protesting about this only the previous month. Councillor Corke was persuaded now that these women needed help, and he urged the meeting to spread the word that it was better to keep a female worker in employment than to dismiss her and put £10 in the Relief Fund.

The Armed Services Sub-Committee, made up of representatives of every armed service agency and chaired by Lady Meux, was overwhelmed in the first weeks of the war, mainly because of the problems with 'allotment'. The allotment of pay by naval men to their families was entirely voluntary. Men had been urged to allot their pay, but ships were leaving port secretly, with little or no notice, usually at night, and many men had not signed the necessary mandates. There were no separation allowances at the beginning of the war either and no pensions for widows or orphans. Within a week the Armed Services Committee had received over 1,000 applications for aid.

Miss Kelly, who would be decorated for her work with service families in Portsmouth during the war, reviewed the activities of the local Relief Committee at a London conference on relief work in June 1915. By this time separation allowances had been introduced for the relations of naval men, contingent however on the allotment of pay through official channels, and a pension scheme was in place. The amount of money they were paying out on a daily basis, she said, had therefore diminished but the number of letters they had to write to the Admiralty and Regimental Paymasters had increased exponentially to some 900 per month as they dealt with the complications of different rates of pay and separation allowances. Maternity work was entrusted to a special committee of ladies who visited all expectant mothers regularly and assisted with advice on insurance matters. They made recommendations to the relevant committees as to relief and clothing, working in co-operation with the Health Department, the School for Mothers, the midwives and approved societies, and with the authorities at the Military Families' Hospital.

The Admiralty and the different regimental organisations notified them of all casualties, and wives and mothers were visited immediately. Grants were administered in the home by almoners, the largest sum paid out in small grants in a single day being £560. These payments also included money for men on sick leave, and they made arrangements for the payment of National Insurance sick benefit, and the provision of light work and training in workshops, and for convalescent treatment. Miss Kelly was also pleased to be able to report on this occasion that the problem of war babies was not an issue in Portsmouth. She had failed to identify even twelve cases. 'Familiarity with khaki', she suggested, 'has bred respect for the soldier.' In short, stories in the popular national press of dissolute behaviour by service wives were wildly exaggerated and not true.

In the meantime, taking a lead from Councillor Corke, local shops did their best to maintain some semblance of normality. They slashed prices and took out advertising in the local newspapers to attract custom. Southsea department store, Knight & Lee, never knowingly undersold then or now, and today part of the John Lewis Partnership, urged parents of young people about to return to school to please make their usual purchases 'and we in turn will quote the lowest possible price for any outfit or single item'. Southsea's landladies were also feeling the pinch. The outbreak of war had a devastating effect on summer trade initially and the *Portsmouth Times* reminded its readers at the end of August that 'Southsea has been and still is quite safe and under normal conditions.' However the paper did concede that news 'that all licensed premises must be closed by 9pm has not helped to reassure possible visitors'. The seafront was also out of bounds.

Significant licensing restrictions were introduced shortly after war was declared. Closing time was brought forward from 11pm to 9pm. This was followed a few weeks later by an order putting all public houses out of bounds to the military until 12.30pm in an effort to cut down on the treating of new recruits. The most drastic restrictions were introduced in early 1916 when Portsmouth and other south coast military areas were brought fully under the Liquor Control Regulations. Opening hours were restricted now to 12am to 2.30pm and 6.00pm to 9.00pm. Orders for spirits to be consumed off the premises could be taken only on weekdays between 12am and 2.30pm; the quantity could not be less than two pints, and the vessel had to have a label indicating where the spirits had been obtained. Credit was forbidden and dilution of spirits to as much as 50° under proof was allowed. 'Treating', literally paying for another man's drink, was banned because of the numbers of young men, recruits and regulars, found drunk and incapable because they had accepted so many free drinks from well-wishers. Punishment was draconian, but the authorities saw this as the only way to stamp out the practice. Offenders risked a £100 fine, several thousand pounds in today's money, and six months hard labour. Not surprisingly there were protests from the licensed victuallers' organizations.

The amount of beer brewed annually dropped by over a half from 36,000,000 barrels to 16,000,000 as did the amount of spirits released from bond. Beer was also significantly reduced in strength. If a publican ran out of beer, he was forced to close until fresh supplies arrived. Prices also rose to absorb significant tax increases. The cost of a half pint tripled from one penny to three pence before falling back to two pence. Whatever the reason, smaller quantities, lighter beers or punitive taxation, incidents of drunkenness fell significantly. Gates reported that during the last two years of the war, there were few cases of drunkenness on the streets.

'Treating' prompts the question why so many young men were keen to enlist. An Anglo-German war had certainly been anticipated for a long time. The race between Great Britain and Germany to build ever bigger and more powerful dreadnought battleships in the years before 1914 was a very potent symbol of an arms race which was unlikely to end in anything but tears. According to Richard Brooks in his book; *Fred T. Jane: A Visionary Eccentric,* the war games at the Portsmouth War Course before the First World War were openly directed at Germany. It could even be argued as well that the invasion of Belgium which did take a lot of people by surprise, and subsequent stories of atrocities, played well with our default xenophobia as a nation. But then again we have to take seriously the idealism which clearly drove many young men to sign up. Former Portsmouth Grammar School boys, like James Yates, who was killed in 1915 aged 26, went to war believing, like the poet, Rupert Brooke, that to be killed was something noble.

It is never easy to fathom motives where they are not clear. Rear Admiral Reginald Tupper's correspondent in one source is a case in point. He clearly tried to use his connections with the Admiral to secure an appointment 'nearer the action'. Tupper was a recent commander of local gunnery training depot HMS *Excellent* and the Portsmouth Division of the Home Fleet. He lived in Southsea and returned to active duty in 1915. He clearly did his best but the Admiralty would not allow 'his young friend' to leave the Paymaster Branch. Dryly, the author of the reply wrote

> 'I could let him[the young friend] go perhaps on the staff of the Officer Commanding a Heavy-Howitzer Battery we are sending to the front if he thinks that would take him nearer the smell of powder and would like it, let me know.
>
> I am afraid there are a good many who wish for the more active side of the war.'

Another young man keen to experience the more active side of things, was Naval Reservist Commander L.G.P. Vereker who would serve with armed merchant cruisers for the duration of the war. On 3 August 1914 he had just finished his bi-annual training, as stipulated by RNR regulations, on HMS *Glory,* a Canopus-class pre-dreadnought battleship, commissioned in 1900, and he had 'gone through' the test mobilization at Spithead. Rumours of war were rife however so he was alarmed to receive a letter telling him to stand by to return to British East Africa, where he was normally posted, at twelve hours' notice. He therefore took the first train to London from Portsmouth to ask his employers, the Colonial Office, for leave to volunteer for service in the Royal Navy which was granted.

The reservists were called out on 4 August and he went straight back to London again, to the Registrar General of Shipping and Seamen at Tower Hill. There he was appointed to Devonport Barracks, and he went home to pack and await further instructions. During dinner that evening at his parents' home, he had a wire ordering him to report that afternoon! He caught the midnight express from Paddington. It was not easy, he wrote, crossing London at that time of night. 'I only just had time… as everyone was so excited as war had been declared at 11.00 pm today.'

Lieutenant Commander Donald MacGregor on HMS *Arun,* a River-class destroyer launched in 1903, expressed the frustrations of many naval men at the failure of the German High Seas Fleet to come out and fight in an undated letter to his mother in Autumn 1914. He wanted 'a crack at the enemy' and some of 'the fun':

> 'The worst of all this is that we all feel so frightfully out of it as these blighters don't seem likely to come out of Kiel so we get all the

bother with none of the fun of fighting. I wish they would get a hustle on as no one is looking forward to the winter in the North Sea.'

He is still complaining to her in a later letter written on 16 November 1914:

'We wish to goodness they would hurry up and come out as this waiting business is very boring. Besides if their destroyers go on getting caught in driblets they won't have any left for us and we naturally all want to have a go at our own kind on the other side.'

In the New Year, he reckoned in another letter to his mother that they had cruised over 15,000 miles since war broke out six months previously and were 'wearing grooves in the sea.'

There is a passage in *Midshipman Rex Carew VC,* a boy's adventure story by John Margerison, published by Nelson in 1920, in which the eponymous hero is making his way by train 'to Portsmouth, HMS *Artemis* and the Great War, where high adventure and romance were stalking hand in hand... .' It is hard not to think that at this early stage in the war this was precisely what large numbers of Portsmouth's raw recruits were seeking. They also enlisted because they believed that it was their patriotic duty to do so. Garbett wrote in the Portsea Parish magazine in October 1914

'It is very difficult to think or write of anything but the war. We all must by now realise that this indeed is a struggle for our very existence as an Empire; and more than this, a German triumph would sound the death-knell of the smaller nations, of treaty obligations, of international honour.'

He therefore urged all able-bodied young men in the parish to ask themselves whether they ought to volunteer. And they did. The following March, he reported that, while it was not possible to give exact numbers of men on active service, he believed that at least 4,000 men had enlisted, and in the St Wilfrid's district alone – it was one of the mission churches in the greater parish - there were over 500 households whose menfolk had enlisted.

For some young men, enlisting also provided an escape from an impoverished existence at home. There is a set of letters in the NMRN which says little about the looming conflict or the author's job on board ship but a great deal about how much he appreciated the food served in barracks and, in due course, on board ship. Stoker Albert Farley was only 16 years-old and had been working in the shipyards of Blyth, Northumberland. His mother was widowed and he had a number of brothers. He enlisted immediately. His letters home to his mother and brothers are glorious accounts not only of the food he ate but of life on board generally for a very young stoker. This is a typical example:

'I am getting on all right with the Bananas salmon sardines Bully Beef Peas Pickel Onions shrimps for tea cocoa for supper Perhaps Fried fish and salmon 2nd course dinner bananas apples Custard and Plums on Sundays I sleep in a brand new hammock just like those in the gardens with on thick woollen Blankett 1 mattress 1 mattress Bolster and all them again in case of washing we use the clean ones. I have 3 Blue serges 4 duck suits 3 hats 1 tooth brush 2 Boot Brush 1 clothes Brush 1 hair Brush and comb 2 [illeg.] drawers 3 bodice flannels everything A1 Meals Plenty to eat eggs marmarlade as thick as you can.'

He had never been so well fed and he had never had such fun. There were free moving picture shows in the canteen and when there were no picture shows, they made their own entertainment:

'We sing and make as much row as the whole of Blyth when the fiddle whistles mouth organs are going send kettle sticks next time you write for I am in the row.'

Other letters describe meals 'of tripe and onions Plenty of cheese and raw onion and cocoa for super at 6.30 and fresh herrings. Spice cake on Sunday. But not as much as you would like.' He spent his pocket money supplementing his rations with purchases made in the canteen of chocolate and penny tins of ham and tongue paste and when they had a good fire below he and his fellow-stokers toasted bread and put on butter and marmalade 'as thick as you like.'

Heart-breakingly for his mother and brothers, he was killed a few months later on board HMS *Natal,* a Warrior-class armoured cruiser, which was sunk after an internal explosion near Cromarty on 30 December 1915 with the loss of 390 crew and civilians who were visiting friends and family. He had not enjoyed his first experiences of the sea particularly, and wrote home just before Christmas

'It is not at all warm on the sea. Look in the dark waters as our ship were coming down only waves breaking up besides our ship then think of home and the fireside I have only found out by now which is the best shelter but never mind. I expect to get home on the new year.'

He was saving hard for his train ticket but hoped he would get a free pass. He thought it possible that his mother would not recognise him when she saw him. In fact she never saw him again. Tucked in with this small cache of letters is the telegram sent to her dated 4 January 1916 telling her 'Regret name of Albert Farley not on lists of survivors received.' A letter from Miss Weston, at the Royal Sailors' Rest in Portsmouth, later in the month, advised Mrs Farley that she would receive her usual allowance for twenty-six weeks and thereafter she 'would get whatever assets accrue from the death.'

Such tragedies hardened the resolve of combatants and non-combatants alike. Equally keen to play their part in the conflict were members of the local volunteer movement. Excluded from military activity for one reason or another, chiefly on the grounds of age, and wanting to do something to defend the country, two local medical men, Dr H. Farncombe and Dr R.J. Lytle, fired with patriotic fervour, rallied friends and acquaintances, similarly excluded, to form a volunteer training corps (VTC) for local defence. Within a few months the new body was well-organised with a chairman and committee. The chairman was artist, Bill Wyllie. Many of these new VTC recruits, like Wyllie, had served in the Territorials before the outbreak of war and they set about the task of recruiting so enthusiastically that within a matter of months they had over 1,000 men, and had engaged Royal Marine artillery instructors to drill them. They had outgrown their original base in the Long Memorial Hall in Southsea and were based now in the Connaught Drill Hall. They brought along their own uniforms which they had made up in a grey-green fabric. The *Evening News* launched an appeal for money for a Rifle and Equipment Fund, and they became affiliated to the Central Association of the VTC. At their first camp at Easter 1915, at Farlington Redoubt, they were introduced, for the first time for many of them, to some of the mysteries of military life which included field evolutions, trench-digging and guard duties.

In May 1916, the War Office put the volunteer movement onto a more regular footing. The local corps became the 3rd Volunteer Battalion of the Hampshire Regiment, and to it were attached VTC detachments in Fareham and Locksheath, Gosport, Havant, Petersfield, Waterlooville and Hayling. The organisation proved in due course to be a useful training and recruiting ground for the 'Regulars', and spawned several satellite organisations of its own: the Volunteer Field Ambulance which provided invaluable assistance to the local Military Medical Service, and particularly to the 5th Southern General Hospital in Fawcett Road; the Volunteer Royal Garrison Artillery (RGA) which did duty at Southsea castle; the Anti-Aircraft Section which manned searchlights and the Hampshire Motor Volunteer Corps which supplied the transport needs of the volunteers.

The women of Portsmouth also threw themselves into the initial war effort. Young women, usually from the leisured classes, raised significant sums of money on flag days and at other fundraising events. A number also volunteered, many as Voluntary Aid Detachments (VADs). The organization was founded in 1909 with the help of the Red Cross and the Order of St John, and became a part of the Technical Reserve of the Territorial Army in 1910. Detachments were established in all parts of the country and training took place which would ensure that in the event of war, they knew what to do. When war broke out, meeting and disembarking the wounded from hospital trains, and driving ambulances, would be an important part of the work of local VADs. Miss Beryl Orde-Powlett motored an astounding 38,000 miles between 1916 and the end of the war, 'without mishap' according to Gates, in a Sunbeam car fitted with an ambulance body. This motor ambulance conveyed some 43,000 patients, usually with Miss Orde-Powlett at the wheel, during its time in service. It was attached to the 5th Southern General Hospital and met all Red Cross trains arriving at Fratton, Portsmouth Town and Cosham stations, and took patients to the hospital in Fawcett Road. VADs also worked as nursing orderlies, cooks, kitchen maids, clerks, housemaids, wardmaids and laundresses, many under the auspices of the Red Cross in local hospitals.

Royal Naval Barracks, c.1910.

One of the most impressive pieces of war work done locally at the beginning of the war was undertaken by a group of naval officers' wives and their friends. They were aware of the problems likely to arise over allotment or, rather, the failure of many naval men to allot their pay. However, those problems proved to be even greater than anticipated. As Miss Kelly and her team discovered, the offices of the Portsmouth Relief Committee at the town hall were overwhelmed with requests for help when war was declared. Local branches of the Soldiers and Sailors Families Association, and the Royal Naval Friendly Union of Sailors' Wives tried valiantly to get in touch with as many sailors' wives as possible but it was feared that many women and their children were being overlooked. Mrs Bradford, the wife of Vice-Admiral Edward Bradford, Commander of the 3rd Battle Squadron in 1914, had volunteered, with Miss Blewitt, daughter of the garrison commander, to give what help they could, and it was Mrs Bradford who suggested that the whole town should be divided into its constituent parishes, and a house to house visitation should take place

Rentals of Houses 6/- to 20/- weekly.   Rentals from 6/- to 10/- largely predominating.

No leisured residents.

Four Clergy of Church of England, very few Ministers of other denominations.

Development of Work

The Vicar of Milton called a meeting of those of his parishioneers who might have some time to spare from daily work and household duties.

Mrs Bradford read an extract from a letter from her husband, Vice Admiral E. Bradford, commanding a Battle Squadron at sea. "So glad you are sharing in the great and useful work that the women have undertaken that is a splendid stimulant to us, it is a relief to all here to think that those who can are assisting those in need".

Seventy of those present undertook to carry out a house to house visitation, each taking a given number of adjoining streets.   Mrs Bradford drew up and had printed a simple registration card, to give name and address of naval man's nearest relation, his rating name of his ship and his official number. (This card was subsequently copied and used in other places and also for soldiers families)

In the course of ten days all houses had been visited, registration cards filled in and returned to Mrs Bardford and Miss Blewitt who with the help of five friends, relations of naval officers, made an alphabetical register of the names received, approximately nine hundred, with particulars.   They made a further list of Streets, seventy five streets in the Parish with names and addresses in alphabetical order for the use of visitors; also register of the names of H.M.Ships, with

the names and addresses of relations of men serving in each
ship. (When the tide of casualties came this was found
invaluable for immediate knowledge of those in trouble)   These
Registers have since had to be increased by a sad record of
widows, orphans and other dependents of men lost on active
service.

Mrs Bradford having been reinforced by five more friends,
every naval man's nearest relation living in Milton was visited
in a very short time.   Many were the troubles discovered.
The main dificulty being the voluntary system of pay to the
wives, which constituted the sole means of subsistence, men had
been in the habit of sending pay home by postal orders, ships
had gone off at a moments notice, no one knew where, no letters
were being received, no money forthcoming.   The wives of naval
reservists were in even worse case, unused to separation from
their husbands, the dificulties were often more bewildering.

Visitors were able to put all cases in need in touch with
relief .   Prompt financial help was given through the H.S.F.A
or other agencies.   Milton being an outlying district
applicants for assistance were often unable to go to the S&S.F.A
Offices at Portsmouth Town Hall themselves, and M R s Bradford
and her helpers were appointed almoners for S & S. F. A and
H. Royal Patriotic Fund, reporting cases to the local committees
and taking relief back to Milton. But verymmany were the cases
where help from relief funds was not needed, though advice,
friendship and sympathy were urgently called for.   The condition
were abnormal, the bewilderment and anxiety great.   One of the
services most frequently rendered and most appreciated was to
put men's wives into touch with the wives of officers serving in
the same ship, a bond of fellowship was formed and confidence giv

Extract from the 'Report on Work in Milton', c.1920.

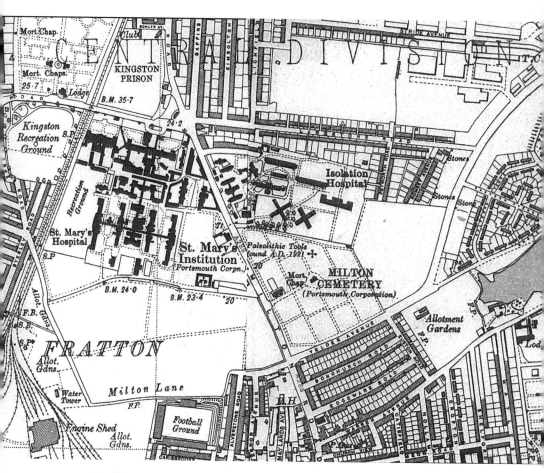

Detail from O.S. 6 inch map of part of the Milton neighbourhood 1858, revised 1932.

in order to register the names of all naval wives. The idea was accepted, and Mrs Bradford was asked to go to the parish of Milton. It was in the south-east quarter of Portsea Island, abutting Langstone Harbour, and had grown up round the new Marine Barracks at Eastney. There were 23,000 inhabitants, chiefly the families of naval men, Marines and dockyard workers. There were few leisured residents.

A useful account survives of what Mrs Bradford and her fellow-volunteers achieved. To begin with, the Vicar of St James's Church, Milton, called a meeting of those of his parishioners who might have time to spare from 'daily work and household duties.' Mrs Bradford read a letter to the meeting from her husband who expressed his pleasure that those present were sharing in 'the great and useful work' about to be undertaken, and that it was a relief to those at sea 'to think that those who can, are assisting those in need'. Seventy of those present at the meeting agreed to carry out house to house visitations, each taking a given number of adjoining streets. Mrs Bradford designed and had printed a simple registration card. There was space for the name and address of the naval man's nearest relation, rating, the name of his ship and his official number. In due course this card would be copied and used widely, and for soldiers' families as well. Over ten days all the houses in the parish were visited, the registration cards were filled in and returned to Mrs Bradford and Miss Blewitt who, with the help of a small team of friends, all relations of naval officers, made an alphabetical register of the names received and their particulars. There were over 900 names. They also made a list of streets, seventy-five in all, with the names and addresses of the residents, in alphabetical order, for the use of visitors, and a register of ships with the names and addresses of the relations of the men serving in each one. When lists of casualties came through in due course this was an invaluable tool for identifying quickly those families which would need help. Sadly, a new set of registers was soon begun too, recording the names of the widows, orphans and other dependents of men lost on active service.

More of Mrs Bradford's friends were recruited next to begin visiting, and in a fairly short period of time everyone registered had been visited. As anticipated, the main difficulty was:

'...the voluntary system of pay to the wives, which constituted the sole means of subsistence, men had been in the habit of sending pay home by postal orders, ships had gone off at a moment's notice, no one knew where, no letters were being received, no money forthcoming. The wives of naval reservists were in even worse case, unused to separation from their husbands, the difficulties were often more bewildering.'

Mrs Bradford and her team were able to put all cases in need in touch with relief through the different agencies. They acted as almoners as well for these bodies, reporting cases and taking relief back to Milton. It was an outlying district of the town and it was not easy for all applicants for assistance, particularly if they had small children, to get to the town hall and the relief offices. Relief funds were not always needed though. Quite often it was advice, friendship and sympathy which were required, and one of the most appreciated services undertaken by the visitors was to put men's wives in touch with the wives of officers serving in the same ship.

Essentially, across the town, through the energy and determination of women like Mrs Bradford and her helpers in Milton, a system was put in place which would endeavour to ensure that no sailor's wife should be without a friend in time of trouble, someone who would help her during the anxious periods waiting for news 'and if bereavement came, to go to her with sympathy and with knowledge of where to turn to for practical help'. In the meantime, money was identified to support a 'resident worker', We should call such a person a social worker today. Miss Marian Edwards, a writer, who offered to come to help in Milton for a few months in September 1914 if her living expenses could be covered. She was still there three years later, and recommending the appointment of a second resident worker in the parish. She gave up much to do this, according to the original report:

> '…and what her personality, her friendship, sympathy and help have meant to the naval population in Milton, especially to those in sorrow and need, it is impossible to over-estimate. She is accessible at all times to those in trouble and no exertion on her part that could serve to alleviate distress has ever been spared. Typical of the feelings towards her was the remark made by a Milton inhabitant at the close of a local debate on "What good can come out of the War." "It has already brought one good in Miss Edwards."

Mrs Bradford met weekly with the women who did the visiting. They hired St Patrick's Institute one afternoon a week for social gatherings, and organized concerts and lectures there free of charge. The registers had to be kept up to date of course, and they also had to discuss and sort out issues relating to naval conditions, ratings, rates of pay, and conditions of service. These had to be understood, and the many new government regulations introduced had to be studied and explained. Overdue changes which took place in autumn 1914 included the introduction of separation allowances for the relations of naval men, contingent however on the allotment of pay through official channels and, most important of all, the first pension scheme.

These developments were certainly not before time. Casualty lists appeared in local newspapers from late August. On 28 August a list was published relating to the naval action in Heligoland Bight and the following week, on 4 September, the first casualty lists appeared from the fighting in France and Belgium. Nearly 5,000 officers and men of the British Expeditionary Force which included Hampshire Regulars were killed, wounded or missing. Two British divisions defeated six German divisions at the Battle of Mons on 24 August but they were forced to retreat; the losses were crippling. The Germans were pushed back between 9 and 14 September on the Marne but here the Allied advance ground to a halt and, almost accidentally, the Germans discovered the advantages of trench warfare. Men in trenches with machine guns could repulse all but the most formidable attacks. On Tuesday, 1 September, the first batch of wounded arrived in Portsmouth, at Fratton Station. There were 120 sick and wounded taken off the train by local VADs. Nine private cars and the Borough Police motor ambulances took them to the hospital installed now in the secondary school in Fawcett Road, today's Priory School.

The Battle of Heligoland Bight on 28 August, the first naval battle of the war, was a victory however. A fleet of thirty-one destroyers and two cruisers under Commodore Reginald Tyrwhitt, and submarines commanded by Commodore Roger Keyes, with cruiser and battle cruiser support, ambushed a number of German ships patrolling their coastline off Heligoland Bight. German losses far outweighed the British and the returning British ships and their crews were acclaimed as heroes by cheering crowds. The engagement had the unexpected effect however of dictating what would happen now at sea in home waters for the duration of the war. Essentially, the German fleet would remain in port, and the war in the North Sea, and in the seas surrounding the British Isles, would be conducted now by their submarine fleet, and through the indiscriminate distribution of mines.

There was a foretaste of this within the month when, early in the morning on 22 September, three British cruisers of the 7th Cruiser Squadron based in Harwich, HMS *Aboukir,* HMS *Hogue* and HMS *Cressy,* patrolling off the Dutch coast, were torpedoed and sunk within just over an hour by *U-9.* There were 700 officers and men of the Naval Reserve, almost all middle-aged family men, many of whom had mustered at Portsmouth, as well as nine cadets from the Royal Naval College, Dartmouth, all under 15 years-old, on each of these ships. 837 men were rescued and 1,397 lost their lives. Young Arthur Layard, still at the Royal Naval College, knew a number of the cadets.

Thousands of miles away, just over a month later, off the South American coast of central Chile, near the city of Coronel, there was more disaster. On 1 November 1914, German Vice Admiral Graf Maximilian von Spee's ships met and defeated the South Atlantic Squadron under Rear Admiral Sir Christopher Cradock. They sank Cradock's two armoured cruisers including his flagship, HMS *Good Hope,* which was lost with all hands. The Germans had an overwhelming advantage in the range and firepower of their modern vessels, and experienced crews. The British ships were obsolete vessels, under-armed and crewed by inexperienced naval reservists. Amongst these young men was E.C. Webber, one of the first of Portsmouth Grammar School's former pupils to be killed in the war. He was a Pay Clerk and the Admiral's Acting Assistant Secretary on board *Good Hope.* He was only 20 years-old. The country was appalled. It was the first British naval defeat since the Battle of Lake Champlain in the War of 1812, the two and a half year military conflict between the US and Great Britain, its North American colonies and Native Indian allies. Once the news arrived, a new naval force was assembled and despatched at once under Vice Admiral Doveton Sturdee.

This expedition would have been in many people's minds when the Mayor of Portsmouth's Annual Banquet for His Majesty's Ministers took place in the town hall. There was a detailed report of the occasion in local newspapers on 13 November 1914. Those present included the Ambassadors of Japan and Russia, the Belgian Minister and French Ambassador, Lord Kitchener, Winston Churchill and the Prime Minister, both in the uniform of Elder Brothers of Trinity House. Mrs Asquith and two of her daughters were also present. 'The country spoke to the world on this occasion, in Portsmouth's Town Hall,' pronounced the *Portsmouth Times.* The speeches were received rapturously by the crowds in the Town Hall Square. They were assured that Great Britain would not sheath her sword until Belgium, France and the other small nations of Europe were restored to their former, unassailable, positions amongst their fellow European nations, and the military dominance of Prussia was destroyed. There had never been such crowds in the streets of the town either for the Mayor's Procession – the 'Khaki Show', as it was called – with local troops marching with men from the Dominions.

Meanwhile, Vice Admiral Sturdee steamed south at speed with two modern dreadnoughts, the battle-cruisers HMS *Invincible* and HMS *Inflexible,* and, off the Falkland Islands, on 8 December, with Rear Admiral Archibald Stoddart, Commander of the 5th Cruiser Squadron, and the survivors of Coronel, engaged and then relentlessly hunted down all but two of von Spee's ships including his two armed-cruisers, *Scharnhorst* and *Gneisnau. Invincible* had its share of naval reservists on board including George Lloyd, Master Mariner, of the Royal Mail Steam Packet Service, serving in what he called 'the giddy and exalted position of Lieutenant RNR'.

His unofficial 'log' of the battle which is in in the NMRN is a vivid account of events. He records the yell of delight from the hands when

HMS Invincible *going into action, Battle of the Falklands, 8 December 1914 from George Lloyd's diary.* **(NMRN 2004.23).**

*Picking up survivors of the Gneisenau **after the action, also showing HMS** Inflexible **and below, visiting the penguin rookery, Port Stanley (NMRN 2004.23).***

the commander informed the ship's company that the enemy was in sight:

> '9.15 Approx. "Action Stations" was sounded and turrets were cleared away. All communications tested and everything as far as possible prepared. The collier *Trelawney* cast off taking with her our two picket boats, 2nd cutter and sailing pinnace. At about 9.30 the enemy's squadron could be seen from the shore consisting of 7 ships, the *Scharnhorst, Gneisenau, Dresden, Leipzig* and *Nuremberg* with two colliers.'

Astonishingly, he had a camera and in his diary are small sepia prints of the engagement including, memorably, the first sight of the *Scharnhorst* and *Gneisenau* on the horizon. The Germans did not know that the British were in the South Atlantic, and Lloyd wrote that they learnt afterwards from survivors that when the Germans saw the British ships they all went to prayers on the *Gneisenau,* and their captain informed the ship's company that they had practically no hope, and were to die fighting. On the *Invincible* they had a 'slap-up' lunch of bread and tongue, and then a chance to stand by their guns and enjoy a smoke for three quarters of an hour. At 1.00pm action was sounded again and they opened fire. The *Scharnhorst* turned over and sank at about 2.30 pm and the *Gneisenau* at around 6.30pm. Lloyd noted what happened. The *Invincible:*

> '…received most of the fire from each ship and the splinters and shell could be heard whistling over us with a peculiar moaning sound. Shortly after the beginning we were struck amidships with a shell which burst in the wardroom and shattered everything the walls being riddled with holes and a great piece torn out of the deck. The explosion shook her from stem to stern. We were also struck by the sick bay wrecking the canteen and setting the sick bay on fire.'

After the 'cease fire' bell at 6.30pm they lowered the boats to pick up survivors in the water from the *Gneisenau.* It was terrible, he recorded;

> '…to see all these fellows in the water. Some drifted close and left their floating supports to try and swim to the ship and although only a few yards, 12ft or so, could not manage it and sank. Some were hauled up a little way and slid down off the lines and were drowned and some the boats picked up. We picked up altogether 105. Seven officers and 98 men; 14 of whom died later and were buried on the following day. The temperature of the water was 42° so that they stood little chance of lasting long. The *Scharnhorst* must have gone down with all hands as all ships were still in action and no one could save them. The German admiral with her. They both went down with ensigns flying and their defeat is no disgrace.'

Altogether, he believed that the enemy probably lost some 2,000 men and four ships to the allies' eight killed and twenty wounded. It was a remarkable achievement. Interestingly, Lloyd talks about his feelings both as they went into the action and during the engagement. Such comments crop up only very occasionally in accounts. He was, he said, 'absolutely indifferent and felt no nervousness whatever, and did not even feel unduly excited'. Fear takes people in different ways. The master-at-arms was reduced in rank to an able seaman, deprived of his good conduct medal and three good conduct badges for being drunk during an action. It was a pitiful sight, said Lloyd, to see a man degraded before a whole ship's company. 'He seemed a broken man and a wasted life.'

Lloyd went ashore at Port Stanley. He visited a penguin rookery, and had a brief walk but the wind was so fierce that there was little pleasure in the exercise. More pleasurable was an invitation to tea on the transport ship, the SS *Orissa*. Christmas was coming and he was given gifts of biscuits, a box of fruit, a jar of pickles and a box of crystalized fruits. He gave them some fragments of German shell. On Christmas Day, the *Invincible's* officers drank champagne in the admiral's cabin before enjoying an excellent lunch. On New Year's Eve, Lloyd wrote, 'What will 1915 bring forth? Good Luck to us and the end of the German Nation, I hope.'

The end of the year in Portsmouth was marked by news of the HMS *Bulwark* disaster which came on top of the loss at the end of November of the submarine E3, the first ship in the Portsmouth Command to be lost. HMS *Bulwark* was a pre-dreadnought battleship which entered service in 1902. She was in the 5th Battle Squadron and attached to the Channel Fleet, patrolling the English Channel. On 26 November, anchored at Sheerness, the ship was destroyed by a large internal explosion with the loss of 736 men. The explosion was probably caused by the overheating of cordite charges stowed near a boiler-room bulkhead. Most of the victims were in the Port of Portsmouth Division. The *Portsmouth Times* was philosophical:

'The town has of late suffered heavily, and widows and fatherless children plentiful, but it is bound to be so, and the country must see that it fulfils its duty generously and thoroughly.'

The paper reported at Christmas that on the whole most of the families of men at war were fairly well provided for by the government and were 'well able' to afford small luxuries for themselves and their children. Most of the shopkeepers were content too and the paper admitted that but for the preponderance of khaki and the lowered lights, it was hard at times to believe that we were engaged in the middle of a fearful struggle. Applications to the Distress Committee at the town hall for civilian relief had also been limited which would seem to indicate that thus far there was not an exceptional amount of distress in the borough.

The town could also celebrate the safe return of Portsmouth schoolgirl, Gwendoline Kyffin, the daughter of local GP and Territorial, Dr John Kyffin. Gwendoline, aged 17 years-old, had been at school in Germany. When war broke out, she was enjoying a trip on the Rhine with two friends. They were separated somehow, the newspaper report does not explain how, and she seems to have been put under house arrest somewhere near Bonn. There she had to report twice daily to the authorities. When she was released, she decided to make her own way home, alone. She walked some 12 miles initially before finally getting a train. The journey took her four days. Apparently, at one stage she found herself in a carriage with five drunken German troops, and in a tunnel a bayonet was pressed into her side, and she was asked whether she wanted to live or die. Somehow she defied the louts – the newspapers do not go into details – and returned safely, finally, to Southsea. She was a local heroine.

CHAPTER 3

The Conflict Deepens

*Antwerp Falls – Portsmouth PoWs – Doeberitz PoW Camp –
Food Parcels – Volunteer War Workers and Depots – Care of the
Wounded – 5th Southern General Hospital, Fawcett Road –
'Brankesmere' as a Red Cross Hospital – Ypres to the Somme –
Dardanelles Campaign – Lieutenant Norman Holbrook, VC –
Gallipoli Peninsula – the Vicar of Portsea's Parish Letters –
Portsea Clergy at the Front – Munitions Shortage – Municipal
College – Women take the place of men in the dockyard and
elsewhere*

Antwerp fell on 10 October 1914. Some 2,000 British troops were
forced to lay down their arms having crossed the frontier into Holland,
and were now prisoners of war. The Germans were free to head south.
They met British troops heading north between 12 October and 11
November in the first Battle of Ypres when trench warfare began in
earnest. New forces were fed into the trenches each day on a narrow
front by both sides until mutual exhaustion set in. The BEF fought the
Germans to a standstill, and itself out of existence. Half of those who
crossed to France in August were now casualties; one in ten had been
killed, three quarters of them at Ypres.

The *Portsmouth Times* reported on 16 October that 200 wounded
admitted to the Royal Naval Hospital at Haslar in the previous week,
their first instalment of wounded, were men of the British Naval
Brigade, and Belgians, who took part in the fighting round Antwerp.
They were brought by rail in two ambulance trains through Gosport to

Royal Clarence Yard where they were transferred into hospital boats and taken down the harbour to Haslar Creek, and thence to the hospital.

The Naval Brigade was part of the Royal Naval Division, formed for service on land from men left over from providing for all present and foreseeable future needs of fleets at sea. They came from the Royal Marines, Royal Naval Volunteer Reserve, Royal Fleet Reserve, and Royal Naval Reserve. A portion were organised into one Marine and two Naval Brigades, the whole comprising the infantry of one division. A graphic account of what he saw was given to the Portsmouth papers by one member of the Naval Brigade who marched to the outskirts of Antwerp from the Channel ports, and then back again. He was appalled by the pitiable sight of refugees.

> 'Who can realise the sufferings of old men and women, bent with age, as they hobbled along the dark and crowded road or the suffering of a mother with a baby in arms and little mites of children crying at her skirts, she too knowing that her husband had given or was giving his life for King and country, or the sufferings of those who had crawled from a sick bed to flee as best they could through the mud and rain, amid the crash of shells and the hustle of the flying crowd or with the sufferings of the young girls and boys who were courageously supporting their suffering elders, though they themselves laboriously bore what valuables and necessaries they could save from their ruined houses?'

The author and his comrades got as far as St Gilles where they entrained for Brugges, presumably to pick up a ship for England, but they did not have too easy a time. Their first ship was a filthy horse transport which ran aground off Dunkirk and they had to be transferred to a South-East Rail ferry. When they got back to Dover, they had been 9 days away, and the writer had never taken his boots off once. The whole enterprise had been chaotic in his opinion, and he did not think that they had been adequately equipped.

At least he got back to England. Other members of the Naval Brigade, many of them Portsmouth men, were not so lucky. Correspondence and yellowing news cuttings amongst the papers of Leading Seaman David Bain in the NMRN relate the experiences of members of the Naval Brigade who were captured near Antwerp and sent to Doeberitz, a large prison camp eight miles outside Berlin. For four days, after they were taken prisoner, they were kept behind the German lines at Laon. They had no food and their overcoats were taken from them. They had to put up with savage behaviour from the German guards who spat on them, and moved them on with the butts of their rifles. On the fourth day, they were packed into coal trucks, seventy-five men to a truck, and sent to Doeberitz where they were interned. There were 3,000 men in the camp. Most of them were English and were captured at Antwerp, although they were joined in due course by French and Russian prisoners. Their treatment was in stark contrast to that of the German prisoners in Portsmouth hospitals at Christmas 1914. The German wounded there were given the same Christmas fare and gifts as the British and Belgians.

Food was in desperately short supply at Doeberitz and men collapsed due to hunger. The scramble for food on one occasion led to the Germans firing into the scrum. A Yorkshire man was so incensed by the shooting of a comrade that he struck the sentry who had fired – and was sentenced to death although the sentence was subsequently remitted to imprisonment. The men were heavily dependent on food parcels from home. The official list asked for tea, biscuits (not sweet), butter (salt, in tin), chocolate, cocoa (or coffee) and milk, bread, condensed milk, golden syrup, jam (tinned), meats (tinned), dried fruits, tobacco, plug, twist and cigarette packs, playing cards and

Preparing and packing food parcels for prisoners of war. **(Portsmouth History Centre 687A/1/3)**.

games, sardines, crushed oats, sugar, oxo, brawn, peas, lentils, soup packets, fish (tinned), tinned vegetables, and soup.

The sending of food parcels to Portsmouth men began in a small way around late 1914 and early 1915, thanks to the efforts of one or two women whose own husbands and sons were prisoners. They worked together unofficially from their own homes. Only in 1916, with the numbers of men imprisoned increasing, and the whole cost of the operation spiralling beyond the ladies' means, was the organization put onto an altogether more official footing. The Mayor, Councillor Corke, agreed to take over the work. The Portsmouth Prisoners of War Fund was established with Councillor Corke as chairman, and a committee was formed. Funds were raised through flag days, collections in schools, churches and work places, at whist drives, and at concert parties and matinées in local theatres. Weekly social meetings were organised by the committee for wives and mothers of prisoners at the St Mary's Mission Hall in Fratton Road. News was exchanged there over tea, and there was musical entertainment. A Christmas party was organized for prisoners' families in 1916 in the town hall. There were over 400 people present, and a photograph was taken. Copies were sent in their parcels to all the men in captivity. Parcels cost 6 shillings each in 1916 which amounted to monthly expenditure of £200. By the end of the war, they had risen to 9 shillings each and were costing £600 a month altogether.

This was a considerable sum of money, raised consistently each month in Portsmouth in addition to the many other fundraising initiatives of local volunteer war-workers, large numbers of whom were women. For many, these activities were useful distractions from worrying about husbands and sons imperilled far from home but they too were inspired by patriotic duty. There was Mrs Charles of Southsea who had been an energetic fundraiser for local charities before the war. She now threw herself into raising money for the war effort. Encouraged by Councillor Corke, she raised significant sums initially for the National Relief Fund in one of the first flag days to be organized in Portsmouth. Fellow-volunteers made and sold tiny, hand-painted Union Jack flags in the streets. She and her team also collected clothing for Belgian refugees who were given sanctuary in the neighbourhood, and when the wounded began arriving at local railway stations, she not only met every train, day or night, and gave out cigarettes and sweets to each man but she also collected cigarettes, tobacco, cigars, sweets and chocolate, handkerchiefs, walking sticks, soap and tooth brushes which were taken to local hospitals.

Another woman who got to work rapidly once war was declared was Mrs Slade-Baker, the American wife of the commanding officer on the Gunwharf. Between them, she and her band of helpers collected sufficient money and materials in the first six months of the war to contribute significantly to ten Red Cross hospitals in Portsmouth and area, and a number of their hospitals in France and Belgium. They sent bedsteads, blankets, sheets, pillow-cases, water-bottles, slippers, dressing-gowns, pyjamas, bed-jackets, scarves, woollen helmets, mittens, boots, overcoats, 'and every other variety of medical and surgical comfort – from bandages to thermometers.' The ladies in the bandage room in fact dispatched over 50,000 bandages and dressings to hospitals during the war.

They operated initially from Mrs Slade-Baker's drawing-room in the official residence on the Gunwharf but this soon became impractical, particularly when they had to store 15,485 sandbags. Colonel Slade-Baker was also posted in 1915 and this forced the issue. New accommodation was found for a Red Cross depot, initially in the High Street and then at 'Broadlands', a large, empty house in Southsea. In due course, goods were sent to hospitals in Portsmouth and the neighbouring county, to regiments at the Front, to the Australian Red Cross, to PoWs, and to the French, Belgian, Italian and Serbian Red Cross.

Some 70,000 sandbags were sent out to the Front in 1915 from a war work depot established by Mrs Arnold Forster in the former Almshouses in Highbury Street in the old town. When the pressing need for sandbags ceased, the ladies working there turned their attention to making and collecting items of clothing and other goods for soldiers and sailors, hospitals and hospital ships. They made shirts and socks, and, like Mrs Slade-Baker's ladies, pyjamas and bed-jackets as well as slippers, trench-slippers, operation socks and pneumonia jackets. They also made treasure bags for wounded men to put their small belongings in when they set off on the often long and tortuous journey from casualty clearing station to nearby hospital and then by steamer and railway, to hospital in England.

The Highbury Street team also produced anti-vermin suits which were made of butter muslin which had been dipped in a solution of Lysol, a popular cleaning and disinfectant product of the time. They were worn next to the skin and were much sought after by the men at the Front sleeping in bug-ridden barns and dugouts. Parcels sent out to ships included jerseys, helmets, mittens, sea-boot stockings, and mine-sweeping gloves with padded palms. Apparently the recipients drew lots for items. As HMS *Canopus* prepared to leave Port Stanley, after the successful engagement against Admiral Graf von Spee, Rating Joseph Bamber noted on 20 December that it was 'Sunday Routine' and afterwards they 'drew lots for more winter clothing sent by Miss Storey (I received a comforter).' This was a Portsmouth parcel.

There was a Surgical and Medical Depot at Lennox Mansions, Southsea run by Miss Bevington. Bandages of all shapes and sizes, swabs and limb-pillows were manufactured here by another team of volunteers. Sphagum moss, with its absorptive and very acidic properties inhibiting the growth of bacteria, was used by the ladies in the preparation of dressings, and it is more than possible that they were delivered to hospitals in France by Mrs Wyllie. In her autobiography, Marion Wyllie wrote that from the very beginning she and her husband started their war work:

> 'I [was] backwards and forwards through France with what, in the end, totalled 89 tons of hospital supplies and comforts for the wounded and suffering. For the first time in our lives neither Bill nor I knew where the other was! He would disappear in one or other of the battleships, and I into France. At these times no news passed between us, and if by chance we saw or came across anything that was secret, we did not even tell each other, or anyone else.'

She had been moved to act when she received a letter in October 1914 from a friend telling her of the dire conditions in two hospitals, one in Dieppe and another in Limoges. The Dieppe hospital had 500 wounded with only two doctors and one nurse to care for them. The men were dying from tetanus, septic wounds and gangrene. Within a week, with the help of friends, Marion Wyllie had packed a number of enormous

bales of medical supplies and was on her way to France with Miss
Bevington on the Red Cross yacht *Medusa,* secured through the good
offices of the Portsmouth Commander-in-Chief's Flag Captain.

The ladies packed bales in Bill's studio. Marion described the scene
when he was at home painting.

> 'He would work at his easel in the window of his studio, surrounded
> by my ladies, grass widows and, alas, war widows – who packed the
> hospital goods as they came in, until I was obliged to place a sofa
> about a yard from his legs to indicate where the packing must stop.
> All this work staved off loneliness and the terrible anxiety.'

For two years she crossed to France every two months with tons of
stores for different hospitals along the French battle line. On one
terrible day, according to Gates, when some 30,000 refugees were
converging on Limoges from Lille and its immediate environs, 10,000
dead, dying and wounded were lifted out of trains in Limoges. Bales
of hospital supplies were also sent out to the Red Cross hospital on
Mudros, the small Greek port on the Mediterranean island of Lemnos
in the Aegean. It was the allied base for the blockade of the Dardanelles
for the duration of the war, where casualties were taken before the
evacuation of the Gallipoli peninsula at the end of 1915. Mrs Arnold
Forster acted as treasurer for the hospital and with the £1,000 the ladies
raised annually, Marion Wyllie was able to send out to them over 90t
of clothing, comforts, surgical dressings, food, blankets, beds and
cigarettes. After the yacht *Medusa* ceased to be available, she travelled
on board hospital ships until the submarine menace put a stop to this
privilege.

Gates was fulsome in the tributes he paid to Portsmouth people for
their care of the wounded in both local, purpose-built, hospitals and in
the hospitals in buildings turned over hurriedly for such purposes.
These included, to start with, the boys' and girls' secondary schools in
Fawcett and Victoria Roads, Sir John Brickwood's mansion,
'Brankesmere', on the corner of Kent Road and Queen's Crescent in
Southsea, and Mr Frank Bevis' large house, 'Oatlands', on Kingston
Crescent. However, in due course, the Royal Hospital handed over
three wards to the military and the Board of Guardians the entire
infirmary at Milton. As the war progressed, and the numbers of

The tessellated pavement in the front porch of 'Brankesmere' and five further images of the house today. **(Phil Parkinson).**

casualties grew, more and more accommodation was needed locally for their care: the Infectious Diseases Hospital, also at Milton, the Eye and Ear Hospital in Pembroke Road and, in the Portsmouth hinterland, establishments in Havant, Emsworth and Petersfield, also on the Isle of Wight. Together they all formed the 5th Southern General Hospital. There were 300 beds at the beginning of the war. By the end there were 2,200, and some 38,000 casualties had been treated. Gwendoline Kyffin's father, now Territorial Colonel John Kyffin, was the commanding officer of the 5th Southern General Hospital at the outset and remained in post until he was sent to Salonica in 1916. He was soon joined by other Territorial officers who were medical men and, in due course, as the need grew, by civilian medical men who were called up. Territorial Nursing Service Sisters were employed initially to undertake nursing work and were supplemented when needed by Red Cross VADs.

The relief hospital set up by the Red Cross in Sir John Brickwood's house was particularly highly thought of. Sir John decamped with his family to his house at Hindhead, Surrey and 'Brankesmere' was handed over for use, initially, by convalescents from the Alexandra Military Hospital. The local newspapers were enchanted with this patriotic demonstration. The patients would have large, warm and comfortable beds, wrote one correspondent, and those who could, would enjoy the sun on the

surrounding lawns. There were five
medical men and six trained nurses.
The boudoir, drawing room, dining
room and bedrooms were all fitted
out as wards with beds, and the
billiard hall as a dining room, for
those able to assemble for meals. The
doctors and nurses, VADs, orderlies
and cooks, all part-time, gave their
services free. The Government
allowed the patients a small daily sum but it did not cover the costs. A
sympathetic public donated the balance of the funds for drugs and
dressings, and for writing paper, envelopes, cigarettes, fruit and sweets.
There were seventy beds to begin with and with tents and, later, huts
in the grounds this number increased eventually to 130. 'Brankesmere'

received principally cot cases and, altogether, 2,385 men were nursed there. The Branksmere orderlies also transported casualties from railway stations to hospitals, and between hospitals, in their very fine Clément Talbot motor ambulance, the gift for the duration of a local well-wisher. Two indefatigable volunteer ladies managed the business of the hospital. Picture postcards survive in several local collections of fundraising ventures in the hospital grounds, and teams of orderlies lined up alongside the Clément Talbot.

The 1st Portsmouth Battalion was not yet at full strength and would not complete its training and be sent to the front until spring 1916. In fact the first two hundred recruits only left Portsmouth for Dublin which was to be their training centre in mid-September 1914 but the Hampshire Regiment sent two regular battalions off to war in August with the British Expeditionary Force. There were many Portsmouth men, professional soldiers, serving in this, the county regiment. One battalion saw service in France and the other in the East and, to start with, it was fairly easy to keep track of their respective movements. There came a time though in 1915 when, according to the author of *The Battle Story of the Hampshire Regiment,* F.E. Stevens, the

authorities, for reasons connected with keeping secret the British order
of battle, dropped a curtain over battalion numbers. After a short while,
they also removed the names of the different regiments from
despatches 'and within a few months the Hampshires were utterly
swallowed in the fog of war.' Although there were veiled references to
'a Southern County Regiment' in official documents it was practically
impossible to pick out battalions in a particular movement.

However, Stevens had a fair idea of what happened. The 1st
Battalion was in Northern France during the early part of the war; the
2nd saw its first service in Gallipoli but subsequently reached France
in time for the great battles of mid-1916. The 8th Territorials were sent
to Egypt after Gallipoli and subsequently took part in the Palestine
campaign; the 10th were in the Dardanelles in the latter part of the
fighting and went on with the 12th to Salonica. Nearly all the Territorial
battalions were concerned in the fighting in the East, the first to go into
action in Mesopotamia being the 1/4th Battalion. The 11th, a Pioneer
Battalion, and the later formations of Service Battalions which included
the 1st and 2nd Portsmouth battalions, went to France, and were joined
there late in the war by the 2/4th, the only Hampshire Territorial
Battalion, apart of course from Territorial troops of other arms raised
in the county, which saw service in France as a whole. In all, by 1916,

Officers of the Hampshire Regiment encamped in winter 1914-15 near Ploegsteert.
(F.E. Stevens, The Battle Story of the Hampshire Regiment).

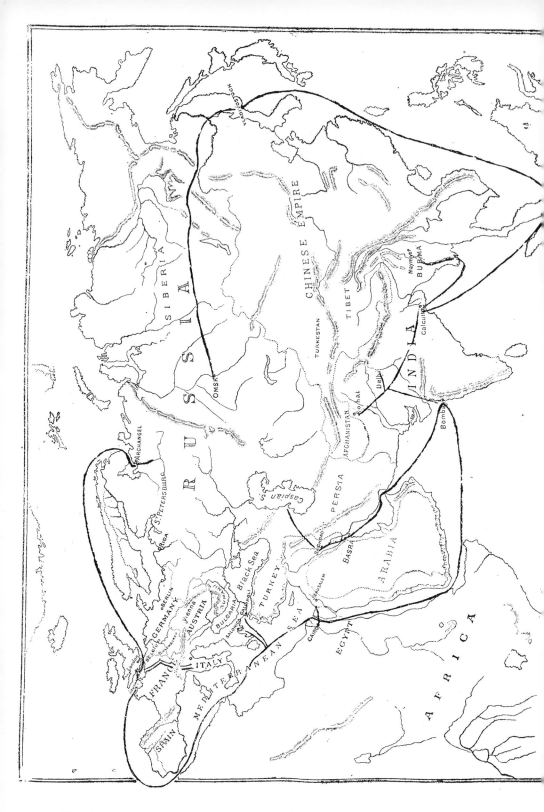

Map showing where the Hampshire Regiment served during the First World War, and where they were in the fighting line (The Battle Story of the Hampshire Regiment).

there were five battalions of Hampshires in France, including the two battalions formed in Portsmouth by Councillor Corke, and his committee. The 14th (Service) Battalion (1st Portsmouth) under the orders of the 116th Brigade (39th Division) landed at Le Havre on 6 March 1916. The 15th (Service) Battalion (2nd Portsmouth) under the orders of the 122nd Brigade (41st Division) landed in France in early May. But this is to get ahead of ourselves.

According to Stevens, the story of the Hampshires from Ypres to the Somme did not differ greatly from the general war story of tedious and monotonous trench warfare. It was impossible to keep track of the different battalions. They lost their individuality.

> 'The regimental records, the log as it were, contained the details, but that of course is little more than a table of dates and place-names. Glimpses are available of course of the minutiae of the Hampshires' experience, but they only help in small degree towards the building up of the picture. There was the alternation of the dreariest of trench routine and billets, varied sometimes by trench digging in the rear and the elaborate preparations which at that stage of the fighting were regarded as necessary to the various shows.'

The Hampshires were dotted all along the line, their position varying from week to week. The men made the best of their spells in the trenches. Their dugouts acquired names, as did the trenches. They took part in patrol work between the lines, undertook the never-ending work of repairing trenches, protected working parties, and occasionally had the thrill of a trench raid. There was even, in Stevens' words, 'an occasional flash of the old order of fighting, like Festubert, Neuve Chapelle, Wychtschaete, Loos and St Eloi.' Presumably this is what he meant by 'the various shows.' Sir John French blamed their failure to make any progress on shortages of shells. Gallows humour was the order of the day and for the most part, those days were made of what Stevens called

> '...small happenings, small that is from the stand-point of men who were constantly under fire, constantly cheek by jowl with death, regularly soaked by the rain and shrivelled by the biting wind.'

Stalemate on the Western Front went hand-in-hand with the frustrations of the Second Front, in the East, on the Ottoman Empire's Gallipoli Peninsula, which formed the northern bank of the Dardanelles. This was the fast-flowing strait which provided a sea route for the Russian Empire from the Eastern Mediterranean through the Sea of Marmora to the Black Sea ports, most importantly Odessa.

As long as the Ottomans (the Turks), stayed out of the war France and Britain could send much-needed supplies to Russia by a sea route which was not ice-bound during the long winter months. The movement of goods overland across Europe was blocked now by the Central Powers, Germany, Austro-Hungary, and Bulgaria. In addition, the Baltic ports were blockaded. Allied access to Russia's Black Sea ports would also allow the Russians to export grain to the west, as a Royal Marine captain said when he gave a lecture to the officers on the battleship HMS *Agamemnon* just before the British and French attempt to force the straits began in February 1915.

Wooed by both sides, the Turks responded finally to the blandishments of the Germans, not the Allies, and entered the war on the side of the Central Powers on 31 October 1914, and the straits were closed. Planning began at once in London and Paris on a scheme for a naval attack the following year, which would clear the strait and allow Allied troops to land on the Gallipoli Peninsula and advance on Constantinople. Such an enterprise might even open a back door into Germany. It was a gamble which Winston Churchill, First Lord of the Admiralty, thought was worth taking.

The enterprise was in fact an unmitigated disaster. The Allies seriously underestimated the strength of the Turkish opposition led by their German officers. The naval attack which was launched towards the end of February 1915 was repelled, the Turks and their defences proving to be much tougher than the Allies expected, and after eight months of heavy fighting on the Gallipoli Peninsula, with appalling casualties, and losses of up to 250,000 men on both sides, the Allies withdrew, evacuating their troops to Egypt. The second front was closed down and efforts were concentrated now on the Western Front. There would be no more distractions or side shows. However, men were kept in Egypt to guard the Suez Canal from possible Turkish attack, and some crossed over into the Sinai Peninsula, ostensibly to make the canal more secure. They encouraged some Arab tribes to revolt against Turkish rule and in due course, at the end of 1917, Jerusalem would fall to the Allies but little harm was done otherwise to the Germans and up to 2,000,000 men were tied down.

The extraordinary deeds of bravery – a Portsmouth story – performed by Lieutenant Norman Holbrook and his crew in the Dardanelles passage, on 13 December 1914, for which he was awarded the VC, looks now more like an isolated event than the opening gambit in what it was hoped at the time would be a short, sharp and successful campaign. Norman Holbrook was 26 years-old and commanded the submarine HMS *B11*, was a former pupil of Portsmouth Grammar School, and the son of Colonel A.R. Holbrook of the Hampshire Territorials, owner of the *Portsmouth Times* and Holbrooks Printers. HMS *B11* was an old submarine, launched in 1906, and was deployed in September 1914 to Tenedos, an island at the entrance of the Dardanelles, at this time under

Lieutenant Norman Holbrook, VC. **(John Sadden Collection.)**

Greek administration, where a British squadron of ships was patrolling the entrance to the straits. The submarine was selected to undertake a daring mission, to make her way up the Dardanelles against the difficult and uncharted current, diving under five rows of mines, to torpedo and sink the *Mesûdiye,* a Turkish Navy 'pre-dreadnought'-type battleship, which was guarding the minefield. The explosion alerted the Turks and the submarine was attacked by gunfire and torpedo boats on the return trip but returned to Tenedos, diving once again beneath the five rows of mines. It took her eight hours, and she was submerged all the way.

Certain key events during the war captured the imaginations of letter writers and diarists. Wherever they are writing, they all note the same disasters and the same triumphs. Lieutenant Holbrook's escapade was a triumph. It was a tonic for the nation. For Arthur Layard, it was also some consolation for the deaths at Coronel the previous month of yet more of his Royal Naval College friends. Other writers were equally dazzled by the story, particularly the writers of juvenile fiction. Percy F. Westerman, the prolific professional writer of boys' stories and, coincidentally, himself an old boy of Portsmouth Grammar School, published *The Fight for Constantinople* in 1915 which can only be influenced by Norman Holbrook's exploits. The Portsmouth newspapers were delighted to report this 'dashing escapade' of a local man, 'the most brilliant since the war began.' It was Portsmouth's first VC of the war and the town was very proud. Norman Holbrook was also the first submariner ever to be awarded the medal, and the first naval VC gazetted since the war began. The mayor and borough council were urged to mark his achievement in some way, possibly by presenting him with an address in a suitable casket.

The appalling losses at Gallipoli also feature in many letters and diaries. It did not take long for the men on board the ships which launched the naval offensive in February 1915 to appreciate exactly what they, and the men they were landing, were up against. An un-named rating, on the battleship HMS *Implacable,* spoke for many observers when he wrote that it was no wonder that we failed to take Achi Baba, the heights dominating the Gallipoli peninsula, despite four gruelling attempts to do so between April and July. He and his mates knew very well that the heights 'were alive with trenches and machine guns in tunnels on rails, and our boys know that it is going to be a tremendous task and will cost thousands of lives.' The offensive did indeed cost thousands of lives. On the battleship HMS *Agamemnon,* the news 'crept through' in late April that total casualties since the landings began were between 8 and 9,000. Elsewhere there were reports of as many as 2,000 men on board hospital ships alongside in Malta on their way back to England from Gallipoli.

Naval and requisitioned merchant vessels were able to anchor off the Gallipoli beachhead only until the arrival of German submarines.

The rating on board *Implacable* had watched in fascinated horror through the rangefinder of a gun on board his ship as 'our troops' advanced on land on the peninsula:

> 'I have never been so excited in my life. A long brown line would suddenly rise out of the shrub and run forward a little way whilst behind them the same thing would be repeated by successive lines of men. After a fairly decent advance the whole line closed on the right and disappeared in a kind of a gully and the same thing was repeated. The way in which it was done in the open was splendid. Shells from the enemy were falling amongst them. Each time I saw a shell hit the ground I would take my head away as I could not bear to see any of our men hit.'

When *Implacable* was sent home finally, he wrote that no one was pleased. They would not be able to say goodbye to the men they had been supporting on land, all of whom were fighting 'like heroes' against overwhelming odds. He lamented the fact that no one at home would ever be aware of the heroism of the boats' crews either. They had run the gauntlet of Turkish fire during landings, went through the same hailstorms of fire when they took supplies onto the beaches for the troops, and went through it all again when they took men off. He reckoned that the men 'out here' were far better informed than those in charge back home. Whatever the end, he wrote,

> 'Victory or Defeat will make no difference. We are the people who know the task that has been set them which in my opinion is more than the people did who is responsible for commencing the operations and I only hope our boys are through before the winter sets in, or else our dear ones at home are in for a shock.'

He was right to be concerned. By the end of November, the crew of HMS *Agamemnon* expected to hear shortly whether they were to take part in an evacuation 'as the conditions are very bad now up in the trenches; men are dying from exposure and there are no billets to fall back into as in France etc.' The commentator reckoned that our troops could be far better employed either in the Balkans or in Egypt:

> 'At present out here things have got into the state that neither side can move, but the Turks only need about a third of the men we do to

maintain their positions. It is not pleasant to think we are leaving thousands of our pals ashore in this Godforsaken hole to no purpose, but such is war, and it's not worth losing any more.'

The 2nd Battalion of the Hampshires distinguished themselves in the fifteen days they were fighting on the Gallipoli Peninsula. According to the report in the *Portsmouth Times* on 7 August 1915, they made a difficult landing, captured a fort and village on the right which was swarming with Turks and machine guns, and on the left captured a hill and amphitheatre which were heavily entrenched and from where there was terrific rifle and machine-gun fire. They suffered significant losses. There are accounts of other battalions fighting for a toehold on the beaches, and the sea turning red with blood.

Temporary Naval Surgeon Fred Gladstone, was completing his six weeks' course at the Royal Naval Hospital, Haslar on 'Naval Hygiene and Discipline' in July and August 1915. As well as attending lectures, he and his fellow medical men, had to look after the patients, most of them wounded men from the Dardanelles. He noted in his memoirs that from Haslar the hospital ships could be seen entering Southampton Water, and when they saw one they knew that in a few hours they would be busy with a fresh influx of wounded.

On the whole, this was light work and they were generally free after lunch when they could play tennis or go into Southsea for a change. To get to Southsea it was necessary to cross the harbour in the hospital picket boat but just before he arrived, there had been trouble. Some young surgeons had spent a riotous night in Portsmouth and fallen into the hands of the dockyard police so a rule had been introduced that all surgeons had to be back in the hospital by 6.00pm which was a great nuisance, giving them time barely to get a cup of tea in Southsea before they had to return home. However, he regarded his six weeks spent at Haslar as really very pleasant, and more like a holiday than preparation for battle in a deteriorating situation.

The vicar of Portsea was particularly concerned at this time by the gravity of the struggle in which the nation was now engaged. Cyril Garbett was vicar of Portsea throughout the war years, and 'The Vicars Letter' in the Portsea Parish Magazines is a remarkable and hitherto unacknowledged commentary both on the war generally and its impact on his parishioners and Portsmouth particularly. He wrote in June 1915

St Mary's Church, Portsea. c.1910.

Cyril Garbett, Vicar of St Mary's Church, 1909-19.

'At first the majority of the people believed that all was going as well as could be possibly wished; that the British Army had won an unbroken series of victories; that early summer would see the victorious and irresistible march of the Allies into the heart of Germany. The hostile Empires were pictured as starving, exhausted and discouraged.'

But recent events were demonstrating that this was far from true, and it was rash, in Garbett's view, for the politicians to keep the public in ignorance.

'The check at the Dardanelles; the serious defeat of the Russians; the delay in the long expected advance on the Western frontier; the fiendish methods of warfare adopted by the Germans, all serve to show that Germany is still immensely strong and absolutely confident of victory.'

Garbett and his staff, 1912. 'Tubby Clayton' is first on the left in the top row.

His own curates' letters home were evidence that the fighting on the Western Front was not going to plan, and that the consequences for the Allied cause were grave. Several had departed now to join the Chaplain General's Department, depriving the Mission Churches in the parish of their dedicated and much loved priests. Philip 'Tubby' Clayton, who founded the club for troops, Talbot House ('Toc H'), at Poperinghe in the Ypres salient in 1915, Sydney Groves, A. Llewellyn Jones and E.F. Edge-Partington, all joined up. Their letters home to the vicar, published in the Parish Magazine, are another rich, hitherto untapped, source on life at the front in the absence of detailed official records. Garbett's curates were remarkable men. Between them, in the course of the war, they accumulated a rich haul of medals for bravery.

They describe graphically the numbers of casualties passing through the clearing stations, and what they do to help and comfort the wounded. They talk of their routine as hospital chaplains, the pitiful cases on the wards, and how they organize church services for their different congregations of patients and hospital staff, the doctors, the sisters, nurses and VADs. Those attached to battalions on the move describe what they see as they travel up to the front line, the devastated countryside, the shattered, abandoned towns and villages, the trenches, the dugouts, and the mud. They describe in detail their make-shift churches, the services they manage to organise in the most unlikely places and situations, and what this means to the men in the trenches, particularly those about to 'go over the top'. These clergymen were frequently under fire themselves, and hazarded their own lives to reach the fighting men. They also recount the occasions when they have to bury casualties for the first time, note the men's details, and the locality of their graves.

The Portsea clergy seem to have arrived in France at roughly the same time, in the middle of the year. 'Tubby' Clayton was sent to the 16th General Hospital, BEF which was at Le Tréport, near Dieppe between 1915 and 1917 when it was taken over by the Americans. The British base hospitals were part of the casualty evacuation chain, further back from the front line than the casualty clearing stations, usually accessible by railway, and near a Channel port. Clayton speaks of a huge hospital under canvas high on the cliff tops, close to the sea. Although the hospital had been in existence for three months there had been no resident chaplain so his first task was to set up a church. He was allotted his own marquee:

> '…and with much ready help – ornaments of local manufacture, an altar of ward lockers, and Communion rails – the handiwork of a convalescent patient, it quickly was transformed into a simple and beautiful church.'

He established a system of services, and his congregations grew week on week. The most popular were his mission services on the cliff top at 7.00pm on Sunday evenings. He also discovered that there were at least two girls from Southsea amongst the VADs.

Llewellyn Jones was attached to the Northumbrian Casualty Clearing Station. It is not clear where. He was one of four chaplains attached to nearby clearing stations and they set up a church together in an abandoned town hall. As word got out that they were there, numbers of medical staff coming to services rose 'most satisfactorily.' He was not able to do a great deal of work in the clearing station as they seldom had patients for more than 24 hours, and when convoys of wounded came in, most effort had to go into feeding the men and dressing their wounds. However, he usually got round most of the wards in the course of the day. They could take over 1,000 patients when 'a rush' was on though he thought their record was 1,200 patients in one 24-hour period after a particularly big attack.

Sydney Groves had a horse and a bicycle to get about with, and he found both 'very useful':

> 'We have a good deal of ground to cover and the roads are by no means ideal. If there has been much rain it is almost impossible to cycle, and the gee-gee is indispensable, but if shells are flying round I personally favour a bike when possible, as you can more easily leave it on the road and take cover.'

He thought it was very important to go up to the frontline:

> 'I think it is a good thing to put in an appearance occasionally. Of course it means going up in broad daylight, and as the communication trenches in these parts are very bad and snipers abound, it is decidedly risky, but I do feel that we chaplains ought to know and experience, even if it is but for a few hours, the conditions under which Thomas Atkins lives in his trench "dug-outs."'

There would always be one infantry brigade resting and he would try to give them an early celebration of Holy Communion before they went back to the front line. Picture, he wrote:

> '...men of all ranks, from Brigadier downwards, kneeling side by side in a barn or under cover of a wood, some of them making it an act of thanksgiving for some wonderful escape from death, all of them feeling it may be their last chance of receiving the Blessed Sacrament'

He tried to organise fairly regular services for the Artillery but there were risks:

> '...it is obviously unwise to collect men in any numbers in an exposed position. German aeroplanes are constantly hovering about looking for our batteries, and if we give the show away and they spot us, it means shells. Shelling over our heads during a service is a common experience, but we are not particularly anxious to get one

in the middle of us. Consequently, we have to be content with a few men at a time, hidden away under the trees. I remember it used to be rather disconcerting when the children let off fireworks through the keyhole during our evening service at St. Faith's, but when these German fellows let off their fireworks – well, I don't think we are cowards, but life seems very precious after all!'

His admiration for the wounded knew no bounds:

'All I can say is that the way they bear their sufferings is perfectly wonderful. Tommy will grouse all day about some minor discomfort, but never about his wounds.'

Ellis Edge-Partington's letters provide some of the most graphic accounts of conditions at the front. Writing on 18 August 1915 'somewhere' in France, he described his brigade's journey out. They left at the end of July, crossing the Channel 'packed like sardines' in their transport 'which made even the regimental dog look gloomy'. After a brief stop on landing at a rest camp, they continued their journey by train – the carriages were horse-boxes – and on foot. Depending on the heat, they made between eight and fifteen miles a day, carrying full packs. He marched with the men and carried his own pack despite being badly attacked by 'the insect life' in the rest camp and suffering 'a bit' from foot sores. Each night they were put in billets, the men in barns and the officers in a farmhouse. When they finally reached their destination, he wrote that now, for the first time, they began to understand the real meaning of war. The town they had reached had been badly shelled, 'a town not much smaller than Portsmouth, and is still shelled a little daily, and as we arrived an aeroplane was being shelled just over our heads'.

They were employed now trench-digging, day and night, marching up in shifts to within a few hundred yards of the first line trenches to dig supports to the reserve line. He took his turn digging, and came under fire for the first time:

'I had been digging, and I was standing up on some raised ground behind with my sleeves rolled up, sweating a bit, for the moment forgetful of where I was, looking on at the others, when suddenly somewhere in front, a shot rang out. It seemed quite close, and a bullet whizzed past my head. I don't think I have ever moved quicker than I did then. Curiously enough my first desire was to get properly dressed; to be shot at in shirt sleeves seemed improper. I also must confess for a bit I had a very queer feeling inside.'

The following day, he buried his first casualty. A party of men digging trenches had massed too much. The Germans caught sight of the group;

'...and put about twenty shells into them in quick succession; it was a miracle only one man was killed. We arranged to bury the body in an hour's time. In the meantime, I took down facts about the man, noted the locality of the grave, and then went round and talked with the other men. I found them wonderfully cheerful and surprisingly little affected by their first and trying experience of shell fire. At 3 pm I took the funeral service; the Brigadier, the officer commanding the party and about 12 men were present. It was an impressive service but a sad beginning.'

By this time, Spring 1915, relentless shelling on the front lines had created a severe shortage of artillery shells, and a major political crisis at home, which led in May 1915 to the creation of the first Coalition Government, the appointment of David Lloyd George as Minister of Munitions and the side-lining, increasingly, of Lord Kitchener from control of military strategy although he would continue to be responsible for the training and equipping of his new volunteer armies. The British Commander-in-Chief, Sir John French, would also resign before the year was out, as much for his part in briefing *The Times* against the Liberal government about the shortage of shells as for failures elsewhere.

Lloyd George's appointment was an outstanding success. When he started work in the London hotel which had been requisitioned for his purposes, there was no furniture and there were no staff. By the time the war ended, the ministry was employing a staff of 65,000, and had over 3,000,000 workers. The army had begun the war with just over 1,000 machine guns. (Apparently, Kitchener thought that four per battalion would suffice.) Lloyd George had some 250,000 manufactured in the course of the war. He also supported the development of the Stokes light mortar, one of the best weapons of the war, which the War Office had previously vetoed, and was responsible for turning the armoured tractors or 'tanks' into practical weapons.

Portsmouth played its part in the campaign to manufacture more shells. The Chamber of Commerce promised to do all that it could to establish munition manufacturing plants in the area and the redoubtable Sir John Brickwood stepped forward once again and donated a large building in Portsea for use as a munitions factory. According to the *Portsmouth Times* on 10 September 1915, as soon as permission had been obtained from the Ministry of Munitions, the work of equipping the building, which would be capable of turning out at least 1,000 shells a week, would begin in earnest.

Training of munition workers became an important part of the Municipal College's war work. A machine shop was created out of a large drawing office and fitted out with the necessary equipment. Recruits were taught general engineering skills, oxy-acetylene welding and electrical engineering. Only men over military age were employed in munitions work to begin with; and after training they began making 18-pounder high-explosive shells. However, in the course of 1916, as the demand for fighting men grew, women took over munitions work

Women working in Boathouse No.6. **(PHC 1338A).**

Women who worked in the Block Mills posing for a group photograph and proudly wearing their triangular badges embroidered with the words 'On War Service'. **(PHC 1351A/1/1).**

from men and after training went into local factories. Altogether the college trained well over 1,000 women.

Another 2,000 women replaced men in the dockyard. They undertook clerical duties initially but in due course, as men went away to fight, had of necessity to be recruited into the different workshops where they proved perfectly capable of doing men's work. In the factory they were employed:

'…in the working of lathes, planing, shaping, milling, engraving, buffing…; in cleaning, cutting, and testing condenser tubes, making condenser ferrules, cleaning air bottles for submarines and ships; in general bench work and assisting the mechanics in cutting blades for condenser turbines. In the Boiler Shop they were engaged in acetylene welding, in cleaning, picking, galvanising, testing boiler tubes. Here also they were employed at lathes, drilling, screwing, punching and shearing machines. They also did small work on forges and assisted the mechanics on the automatic machines for bolts and nuts.'

Women also worked in the Gun-Mounting Shop where, in addition to general bench work, they were employed drilling, shaping, screwing and engraving machines, and in fitting and adjusting rangefinders. They did more acetylene welding in the Coppersmith's Shop, also cleaning and picking tubes, repairing lamps for ships and general work assisting the mechanics. They made packing cases in the Pattern Shop, painted patterns, and turned wood plugs for boiler tubes, made rollers for drawings, and used the band-saw machines. Women also worked in the Drawing Office where they did tracings of drawings and worked associated printing apparatus. On top of all this, they were employed driving capstans for the movements of ships in basins, drove motor lorries, made overalls and flags, undertook electrical work on board ships, lacquered and zinc-coated baths, cleaned and painted the hulls of ships, sharpened saws and worked in the sawmills.

There was some anxiety initially about how easily the women would be integrated into the male workforce. Initially they had to take considerable abuse from their male counterparts. There were taunts, and there was hustling and pushing on the way into work. One woman recalled many years later that it was as well to carry an umbrella with you on the trams 'to give as good as you got.' To start with, the women left the dockyard at the end of the day in advance of the men but this distinction was eventually dropped. At the end of the war many women spoke of this being the happiest time of their lives. They had some money of their own, were respected for what they did and they were proud – of the badges they wore for doing war work and of the fact that they could actually do what was often very hard work. However, as now, it was often very hard if you had a family at home and a husband away fighting to balance the demands of both work and child care. Those with babies spoke of going home in their lunch break to feed the baby. Others had to employ a neighbour or friend to get their children up and off to school.

By the end of the war, 1,200 vessels had been refitted in Portsmouth dockyard. These included forty battleships and battlecruisers, twenty-five cruisers, over 400 destroyers, 150 torpedo boats, 140 trawlers and drifters, twenty submarines and other vessels. During this same period, 1,658 war vessels were docked or hauled onto the slipways for repairs. Most urgently, warships had to be fitted with anti-torpedo bulges and, after Jutland, improved armour plating, as the relative weakness of British armoured plating had been exposed during that battle. Interestingly, troops were never embarked at Portsmouth unlike Southampton with its long-established pre-war passenger transport trade. Portsmouth dockyard was used instead to ship equipment such as guns, tanks, railway locomotives, ammunition wagons and military trucks to the different fronts, and it was not unusual to see long lines of trucks and other equipment being taken in convoy into the dockyard or assembling on the huge parade ground behind the Victoria Barracks.

Women were also taken on at the Army Ordnance Department at Hilsea and at the Gunwharf, working here for the Admiralty. The work at Hilsea consisted of tent repair, and salvaging clothes and bedding, and at Gunwharf making different types of equipment and looking after stores. Women took over other work locally as well, in areas which had been considered the exclusive preserve of men. They went to work as clerical officers in the town hall, and were employed as drivers and conductors by the Tramways Committee. At the Post Office, women were employed to deliver letters, and as telegraphists and telegraph messengers. They also went to work as bank clerks. By the end of the war, according to Gates, they outnumbered men by five to one behind the counters of local banks 'and were doing the most important work with the ease, accuracy, assurance, and secrecy which had been considered the exclusive accomplishments of the male bank clerk.'

By Autumn of 1915, the war was costing £35,000,000 a day; 3,000,000 men had joined the forces, and 600,000 people were now employed in munitions. How on earth was expenditure on this scale – of money and human resources – to be sustained? The *Portsmouth Times* calculated that all of this was on top of a rise in food prices of 40 percent, and a general rise in the cost of living of 30 percent. This had prompted many trades and occupations including men in the dockyard, as early as Spring 1915, to demand higher wages and war bonuses. In February 1916, some 250 borough council employees finally went on strike because the council refused to pay the bonus demanded. The council recruited other men to keep essential services running, and promised to give them permanent employment afterwards. Consequently, the strike collapsed within two weeks and many of the strikers were put out of work. Eventually the council was forced to pay the bonus of 1 to 2 shillings a week with 6 pence for every child under 14 years-old to each of its employees. Not surprisingly news of this sort of unrest at home did not go down well with men on the front line.

The government did try initially to promote taxes against rising expenditure in an effort to keep the costs of living down. Income tax was increased to 40 percent and exemption went down to £130. Increased duties were imposed on tea, sugar, tobacco, coffee and cocoa. There were higher postal charges. A new tax, an excess profits duty of 50 percent, was levied on any increases on pre-war profits, and a duty of 33 percent on luxury goods such as motor cars, clocks and watches. The council itself purchased £8,000 worth of War Loan.

Christmas Day 1915 was warm and damp in Portsmouth. Local churches were well-attended, and treats were organised for all the wounded and hospitalized troops. Happily there were very few people in the Workhouse this year, noted the *Portsmouth Times:*

> '...due to the abnormal labour conditions which have made the working classes more prosperous just now than they have been in all probability at any previous period in our history.'

At the Front, Ellis Edge-Partington celebrated Christmas with the British Expeditionary Forces, in their billets, to their immense relief. The weather was very similar to the weather at home. Before they had left the trenches, he had seen a fine holly tree 'more red than green so great were the number of berries upon it'. He cut off a number of the best branches, and had them taken down to the billets. There, with the help of the regimental bandmaster and a volunteer choir he organized carols which they performed on Christmas Eve at Divisional HQ and Brigade HQ, at their field ambulance, and in three nearby villages where their efforts were greatly appreciated. They had the use of a village schoolroom for a church and he borrowed an item of oak furniture from a neighbouring house to use as an altar. On the wall above his altar he and his team of helpers hung a piece of material the colour of old gold, in the centre of which they placed a fine cross made of the holly. They laid some white linen on the altar, placed their brass cross in the middle, and the candlesticks and vases either side. They then decorated the room with the remains of the holly - and were very pleased with their efforts. Christmas Day was fine and mild. At the first celebration of the day, at 6.30am, he had seventy-two communicants, to his great pleasure.

> 'It was a beautiful service, at which we sang the best Christmas hymns to the accompaniment of a piano. It was quite dark, so the room was lit in front by the candles on the altar and behind by two acetylene lamps.'

At home Garbett, wrote at the end of the year that he believed that the nation was reconciled at last to the fact that this war could not be won without significant sacrifice. Now we knew what we were up against, he said;

> '…we understand that the war cannot be won unless every citizen joins in the task of defending the heritage which has been handed down to us, and of upholding the ideals for which we believe we are fighting, as opposed to an imperialism which is based on brute force.'

He could not know as he penned these paragraphs that Portsmouth would be tested now almost to the limit of its endurance.

CHAPTER 4

The Full Horror of War

Compulsory Military Service – Local Appeal Tribunal – Conscientious Objectors – Saxe-Weimar Road – Jutland – HMS Hampshire – Battle of the Somme – Zeppelin Raid on Portsmouth – Milton Home Industry for Naval Widows

The year 1916 was Portsmouth's *annus horribilis*. Six Portsmouth ships, the battle-cruisers HMS *Queen Mary* and *Invincible,* the cruiser HMS *Black Prince,* and the destroyers HMS *Ardent, Fortune* and *Sparrowhawk,* were lost at the Battle of Jutland on 31 May 1916 and, as noted at the beginning of this book, 4,000, mainly local, men were lost and 1,500 homes left fatherless. HMS *Hampshire,* which hit a mine and sank off the mainland of Orkney in mountainous seas less than a week later carrying Lord Kitchener was another Portsmouth ship. She had a complement of 655 officers and men, and of the three voluntary battalions – of 1,100 men each – which marched off so confidently to Portsmouth Town railway station the year before to complete their training elsewhere, not one returned. Those of the men who survived the carnage of the fighting on the Somme which began on 1 July 1916 were assimilated in due course into the depleted ranks of other regiments. At the end of the year, to compound the horror, there was a Zeppelin raid on the town.

The year began with the introduction of compulsory military service for unmarried men between the ages of 18 and 41. It was possible to appeal and the Local Appeal Tribunal sat in the town hall under the presidency of the Mayor, Alderman Sir John Corke. According to

Gates, the decisions of the tribunal 'were invariably marked by a just appreciation of the merits of each case, the claim of the nation to the services of every capable man being kept steadily in view'. The tribunal would meet on almost 200 occasions over the next three years, and deal with nearly 8,000 applications for temporary or conditional exemption.

Lengthy reports of meetings of the tribunal appeared in the local papers. Early cases included the master builder who said he had a widow and two sisters dependent on him. His three unmarried brothers had gone away to fight already, and he had been rejected by the navy on the grounds of defective eyesight. The military representative present said that this was no longer such an issue on account of close-quarter fighting. The appellant was sent to the Medical Board in Winchester. Another man's claim was based on the fact that he supported a widowed mother. He asked what her position would be if he was killed, and was advised that it would be the same as it would be if he died a natural death. He protested that this was very unfair as the widow of a soldier received a pension. A taxi-cab proprietor appealed on behalf of one of his drivers. He had already lost nine out of ten men and was finding it very difficult to replace them. He was advised to look for older men and discharged soldiers. Applying on behalf of their young (male) corset cutter, a local firm said it now had only four machine cutters left for five factories, employing about 1,200 people. The cutters were working until 10.00pm each evening to keep things going and the appellant said that if they lost the appeal, it would mean closing down part of the works. It took twelve months to train a cutter but if they could have two months exemption, they would be able to 'work something out'.

The tribunal was sympathetic to the need to keep local trades in business. This issue was referred to again in connection with an application from a hairdresser who asked for time to dispose of his business which had been established by his father nearly forty years previously. It was a very good business but he was unable to sell it or find a manager. Other cases included young men who claimed that their mothers' health was frail. They were seldom granted exemption. However, the tribunal was sympathetic to any pleas put forward of genuine financial hardship. They would review cases and defer decisions. There was the case of another hairdresser carrying on a business on his own who stated that he would suffer a serious loss of capital if he was called up. He was just married and his parents lived with him and his wife. His father was in receipt of only 7 shillings a week and army pay would not be sufficient to meet the appellant's expenses. He had paid £69 for his business. It was agreed that this was a hard case. Temporary exemption was granted and the case would be reviewed at a later date. The tribunal was sympathetic similarly to a young taxi-cab driver who was the sole supporter of his mother and sister. He had three brothers already in the navy and his youngest brother, an apprentice, was waiting to be called up. He had begun his business with one taxi when he was 19 years-old. He was now 26 and owned three taxi-cabs and a motor lorry. The claim was adjourned for further inquiries.

Altogether over 4,000 exemption certificates were issued. The tribunal also dealt with applications for exemption from conscientious objectors. The members were never particularly sympathetic. A young man with a stationery business in the Arcade (Commercial Road) appealed initially that his business would be adversely affected if he was conscripted, and that he had an elderly and infirm parent. He also had a conscientious objection to combatant service. He was asked whether he objected to paying his taxes, and replied that there was no alternative. 'Neither has the Military Service Bill any alternative,' said a member of the tribunal. The next question was to do with how long he had been a conscientious objector. 'Just two or three years,' was the answer given, and in reply to a further query as to whether he belonged to any particular sect, he replied 'I have no religious views. I think that religion and war go hand in hand.' He objected as well to taking the military oath because he claimed that it necessitated swearing blind obedience, and this he was not prepared to do. The tribunal was irritated and the following exchange ensued:

'If everyone took this view there would be chaos.

'I owe to man and humanity alone a conscientious allegiance.

'If you owe an allegiance to humanity you surely can have no objection to serving in the Army Service Corps?

'I have an objection to taking the military oath.

'That is not a conscientious objection to warfare.

'It is an objection to warfare because the army is warfare.'

The application was refused.

A Petersfield man was more successful. At a meeting of the Hampshire Appeal Tribunal meeting in Portsmouth Town Hall, Reginald Roper, aged 40, a schoolmaster, appealed the decision of the Petersfield Tribunal to refuse him exemption as a conscientious objector. He objected to any form of military service, arguing that as a schoolmaster he was engaged on work of national importance. He had taken the same position at the time of the Boer War, and had spoken publicly on the subject at the time, preaching sermons and giving addresses against war in general. And yes, some parents had objected about his views. His sister, Miss Roper, said that her brother had held these views all his life – that war was against the teaching of Christ and unjustifiable. The military representative asked Roper what he would do if his sister was attacked and he said that he would do what she would expect him to do, not to protect her at the expense of another man's life! He was also questioned as to his objection to helping the sick and wounded as a member of the Royal Army Medical Corps. He said that he had no objection to helping the sick apart from the machinery of war. To put it bluntly, he considered a growing, healthy child was of more value to the state than a wounded man. Interestingly, when the result of the appeal was announced, there was applause from members of the public present.

More predictable was the movement by local residents gathering momentum now to change the name of Saxe-Weimar Road, Southsea to Waverley Road. The *Portsmouth Times* suggested that while the borough council was at it, they might as well tackle the problems of Angerstein Road, Coburg Street, Gruneison Street, Sultan Road and Turk Street in Landport, Brunswick Row, Hanover Place and Hanover Street in Portsea and, in Southsea, Blenheim Street, Brunswick Street, Heidelburg Road and Kassassin Street. Whether facetiously or not, the newspaper reported that the residents in those streets were just as patriotic as the residents of Saxe-Weimar Road and might also like a more British-sounding street name.

The same edition also reported that official film of our fighting forces was being shown at the *Theatre Royal* to packed houses. There was footage of recruitment for Lord Kitchener's Army, scenes of the new troopers training, a review of the men by the King, and their departure for the Front. There was also film of the Grand Fleet in the North Sea, life on board the very latest battleship, HMS *Queen Elizabeth,* and a feature on submarine warfare. The public were desperately keen for news and expected it, even heavily censored reports. Fast communications were in their infancy but whereas, a hundred years before, news of Nelson's victory at Trafalgar and his death took nine days at sea on the schooner HMS *Pickle,* and 37 hours in a hired post-chaise from landfall in Falmouth, to reach the Admiralty in London, news of the long-anticipated clash between the British and German fleets in the North Sea was now received in official quarters immediately through wireless telegraphy.

The Battle of Jutland was the largest naval battle and the only full-scale clash of battleships in the war. It was a curious sort of engagement. It was not the decisive battle fought at Trafalgar by Nelson's ships. In fact, initially, the Germans claimed that they had won a great victory but this was only because their version of events, confusingly for the British public, hit the news-stands first. Signal intercepts had informed the British that the German High Sea Fleet was planning to lure the Grand Fleet into an engagement and so, hopefully, break the British sea blockade of Germany. However, before the Germans could manoeuvre their ships and submarines into position, and before the British Grand Fleet had met up with him, Vice Admiral Beatty's battle-cruiser squadron fell in with Vice Admiral Hipper's five modern battlecruisers. The *Portsmouth Times* took up the story. The Germans had the advantage of light, visibility, numbers and position but this did not deter our men who fought with distinction throughout, it reported. The Germans were also within easy distance of their own coast. When Admiral Beatty took up the challenge:

'…he had at his disposition a fast squadron of battle cruisers and armoured cruisers – 14 ships in all – with the North Sea between him and his home ports. And the type of cruiser with which he was fighting was designed for great pace, and chiefly for fighting a running battle at long range, and was not the ideal force with which to stand against the whole weight of the German Battle Fleet – the work of Dreadnoughts and super-Dreadnoughts. Sir David Beatty saw the risks and deliberately took up the challenge of the German fleet, and though at the outset out-numbered 7 to 1, engaged the enemy, and with wonderful gallantry and tenacity held them all till Admiral Jellicoe came up. Over weighted at the start, the British continued the fight with the advantage of light resting with their opponents, who made full use of it. As the sun set, the British ships were silhouetted against the horizon, and they were only able to fire at gun flashes, the Germans being veiled in mist. And when at last the British Fleet came in sight, with the Iron Duke leading, the enemy found the tables turned, refused to continue the engagement and ran for home.'

As for German claims that they had won a victory, the *Portsmouth Times* was scathing. It was a strange commentary, it stated;

'...on the claim of a German victory that the British Fleet remained in possession of the field of battle, and traversed it until, finding no enemy to attack, it returned leisurely to its bases to refit. A few hours later the 'defeated' British Fleet was again ready for action.'

All the unofficial diarists and letter writers talk about the odds stacked against Beatty and his ships and how, in the circumstances, between them all, they fought a brave battle and that those who died did not die in vain. Knightley Boase, a young officer on board HMS *Inflexible*, wrote initially to his family, in Southsea, on 3 June to assure them that he was well and 'in the land of the living':

'All's well that ends well and though first press reports were gloomy reading there is no need to worry and I am confident that the German rejoicings and flag waving were extremely premature and that their 'glorious victory' was not obtained on May 31st. Undoubtedly we have suffered very heavy losses and it is dreadful to think of all those families which have been so cruelly stricken but they did not die in vain and I believe absolutely that when the truth is known we shall then realize that the German victory was in reality much nearer a defeat. Weather conditions were greatly in their favour as the Press messages state but I cannot say more now.'

A few days later he went into more detail in a letter to his brother, George. 'Our squadron mates' in the battle cruisers, he said, did not die in vain;

'…we are all perfectly certain that we did much more damage to our opponents than they did to us. It is an undoubted fact that they scored heavily at first by the weather which was very hazy and they had our ships against the western sky and it was then that they caught the *Queen Mary* and *Indefatigable* but they never really faced the battle fleet at all and I am convinced that with clearer weather we should have had an overwhelming victory. As it is there is no doubt that the Germans lost very heavily but we must wait for the C-in-C's report before we can say more. As to our part in the action I can say only that we bore our share of the fighting and that we were lucky to escape without casualties at such close range. Our own flagship – the *Invincible* – lead us in magnificently and it was a sad moment when she ended her career and left us to lead the line for we had many friends on board and it is a marvel how anyone could have escaped. We had pretty warm periods with gunfire, torpedoes etc but I believe the *Invincible*'s opponent had a very much warmer experience from us. It was a fine sight to see our battle fleet come into action and we were pretty glad to see them, but the honours go chiefly to our destroyers for they were handled magnificently and did excellent work. It was pretty gruesome later on to recross the battle area as we passed hundreds of bodies – but nearly all Germans.'

He wrote to his mother on 11 June about 'our scrap off Denmark'. He knew many of the people who went down on the HMS *Queen Mary* and HMS *Indefatigable*. He and a colleague on *Indefatigable* had examined twelve of the midshipmen on board the *Queen Mary* a few weeks before 'and now all have gone except a few midshipmen.' 'War is a gruesome business,' he continued, '…and one feels so desperately sorry for all the widows and relatives. From our own nearest village some twenty officers' widows have left and we miss many familiar faces. It is all so horribly sad although their husbands died in a good cause.'

He was too busy to be frightened during the action. There was one anxious moment though when a torpedo went down their port side about 20ft away. But, like so many of them who went into battle that day, it was the heroics which captured and thrilled their imaginations. It was such a fine sight, he told his mother;

'...to see our own battle fleet come into action and the sides of the battleships vomiting out flame and smoke, but they did not get much of an innings as the Germans showed wise discretion and went home hurriedly. Our destroyers were simply marvellous and made most daring attacks by day and night; they suffered rather heavily but did an immense amount of damage.'

For sheer heroics at Jutland however little could beat the bravery and sacrifice of former Portsmouth Grammar School boy Major Francis Harvey whose actions prompted Winston Churchill to comment later that in the 'long, rough, glorious history of the Royal Marines there is no name and no deed which in its character and consequences ranks above this.' A gunnery expert, Harvey was senior Marine officer aboard HMS *Lion,* the 27,000-ton flagship of the British battle-cruiser fleet commanded by Admiral Beatty. The battlecruisers led the initial British attack on the afternoon of 31 May 1916. *Lion* was hit mid-afternoon by nine shells, one of which penetrated Harvey's 'Q' gun turret, killing or wounding everyone inside. Mortally wounded in the explosion, he realised that, with the damaged hatch in the turret now wide open, flash-fire could travel rapidly to the magazines below. Before collapsing, he managed to send a message down the voice pipe ordering the magazines to be flooded, to prevent the tons of cordite from detonating catastrophically and destroying ship and crew. His action that day saved the lives of at least 1,000 men. He himself died shortly after and his body was buried at sea with full honours along with the other ninety-eight casualties. He was posthumously awarded the VC which his widow, Ethel, received from King George V at Buckingham Palace on 15 September 1916. His medal group is today in the Royal Marines Museum, Eastney.

Temporary Surgeon Fred Gladstone was also at Jutland. After his 'six pleasant weeks' at the Royal Naval Hospital, Haslar, he was posted to HMS *Centurion*, one of the very latest 'super-dreadnoughts'. He was fortunate. The man in front of him on the list posted in the Porter's Lodge at Haslar was appointed to HMS *Invincible* and lost his life at Jutland, and the surgeon below him on the list was appointed to HMS *Natal* and lost his life when the ship blew up at anchor in Cromarty Firth on 31 December 1915. Like George Lloyd in the South Atlantic in 1914, Gladstone had a camera on board *Centurion.* He recorded rare

'The Lion Roaring.' A picture postcard of HMS Lion in action, presumably at Jutland. The ship survived the battle thanks to the gallant action of mortally-wounded former Portsmouth Grammar School pupil, Major Francis Harvey.

leisure opportunities, like the picnic on the rocky Scapa shore, and midshipmen, in time-honoured tradition, sailing a whaler from one of the battleships. There are also photographs of HMS *Erin* and HMS *Agincourt*. Both ships were originally ordered by the Turkish Navy but were still under construction when war was declared. They were subsequently seized by the British Government, renamed and put into service with the Royal Navy where they both saw action at Jutland. Gladstone wrote in his memoirs, as have many historians, that this was a contributing factor in the Turks' decision to enter the war on the side of the Central Powers. They had, after all, paid for the ships in full. However, this theory is disputed today in some quarters as a secret alliance had been agreed between the Turks and the Central Powers before 4 August 1914.

Apparently Gladstone's squadron – the Second Battle Squadron – which came from Cromarty met up with the Grand Fleet mid-morning on 31 May. Like Knightley Boase, Gladstone also reckoned that the Grand Fleet at sea was one of the finest sights that he had ever seen:

'…some seventy-five great dreadnoughts moving through the water in perfect alignment, accompanied by their attendant hosts of

Forecastle, HMS Centurion, *1916.* (Gladstone family).

Quarterdeck, HMS Centurion,
1916. (Gladstone family).

The wreck of HMS Natal,
Cromarty Firth, 1916.
(Gladstone family).

HMS **Iron Duke** *at Scapa Flow, 1916. Built at Portsmouth and launched in 1912, she was the flagship of the Grand Fleet during the First World War including at Jutland.* (Gladstone family).

Picnic at Scapa Flow, 1916. (Gladstone family).

Whaler and midshipmen at Scapa, 1916. (Gladstone family).

HMS Erin, *1916.*
(Gladstone family).

HMS Agincourt, *1916.* (Gladstone family).

The sick bay, HMS Centurion,
1916. (Gladstone family).

destroyers and light cruisers, the greatest naval force that ever put to sea, made a spectacle that never failed to thrill.'

Waiting for action, they made sure that their dressing station, or medical flat as it was called on board ship, was in the correct state of readiness. They then went for tea in the wardroom. He could not help reflecting that they were in a very different position to the army. Here they were sitting down to an ordinary tea in very ordinary surroundings and at the same time expecting every minute to be engaging the German Fleet. The nervous tension caused by having to wait, 'with nothing to occupy the mind and without the slightest idea of what was taking place was most trying.'

They passed the wreckage of the *Invincible*. On board the *Centurion*, they thought it was the wreckage of a German ship although their captain who had been in command of *Invincible* thought he recognised the stern of his old ship. Time went by very slowly 'and there was little to be done except to wait and wonder what was going to happen next'.

The Battle of Jutland, 31 May 1916. **(Gladstone family).**

Centurion opened fire finally at 7.15pm with her main armament. As full charges were being used, Gladstone recorded:

> '...the concussion was tremendous, and the whole ship vibrated and heeled over as the guns went off. Clouds of dust disturbed by the concussion came down the ventilating shafts, with the result that the atmosphere in the flat, already bad, was made infinitely worse and it rapidly became impossible to breathe.'

Admiral Hipper now directed his battlecruisers at the British battle line in the hope that in the ensuing mêlée this would create, the rest of his fleet could pull away to safer waters. They met such a barrage of fire however from the Grand Fleet that they rapidly became a shambles and ran away in order to escape total destruction, and from then onwards 'the fighting, as done by ships of the Grand Fleet, gradually died down and was never renewed to any extent'. Gladstone comments that below decks, in the medical flat, they did not have much idea of what was going on. The battle was fought at such speed and over such a large area of sea that it was quite impossible for any one person to understand exactly what was happening. In the meantime, they had hurried drinks and sandwiches in the Ward Room before returning to their respective battle stations. There was great fear of German attack at night as German destroyers enjoyed an enviable reputation for night work 'and it was felt that we would be very hard pressed to keep them off. The strain now, in the middle of the night, was very great indeed'.

He recorded that at around 1.00am there were flashes, and gunfire was heard astern. German battleships had run into British destroyers which were themselves stationed astern of the battleships of the Grand Fleet; it was the German High Seas Fleet crossing the rear of the line. They had run into some of the British light cruisers and destroyers sailing at night cruising stations three or four miles behind the battleships. 'It was here', said Gladstone, 'that some of the fiercest fighting took place during the night and the small hours of the morning'. To their chagrin and disappointment, the Germans finally slipped away. The next day some of the ships held burial services and buried their dead. Only when they saw the newspapers did they understand that there had been a major naval battle and casualties in ships and men had been very heavy.

Over the next few days, the number of letters needing censoring on *Centurion* became enormous, wrote Gladstone. Everybody, it seemed, wanted to become an author, and many of the letters contained graphic accounts of events which had never actually taken place.

> 'Fortunately for the sake of future historians, all these dramatic accounts had to be ruthlessly cut out, with the result that most of the letters took on a very tattered appearance… Personally I contented myself by sending a postcard home on which I wrote "Alive and well".

Fred Gladstone was lucky. Gates described graphically how the first news of the battle reached Portsmouth. It was shortly before 7.00pm on the evening of 2 June. There was a warning tick on the telegraph machine in the *Evening News'* offices which indicated that a message was about to come through. The words 'GREAT BATTLE IN THE NORTH SEA' were flashed through and then, with mounting horror, the staff which had not yet gone home read the Admiralty despatch listing the ships lost, most of which belonged to Portsmouth. The news spread rapidly. Never, said Gates, had there been more distressing scenes witnessed in the town that night. Miss Kelly and the Armed Services Committee team, known generally now as the Service Committee, worked through the night to render what help they could to women in distress. Their offices in the town hall were besieged by people anxious for information or assistance. It was Miss Kelly who calculated then that the loss of Portsmouth men would be in the region of 4,000, and 1,500 homes would be left fatherless. Members of the Service Committee set about visiting each widow in her home. They were able to assure the widows that the Admiralty would continue to pay separation allowance, as before, for six months and by that time, pensions would be ready.

An account survives of the activities of Mrs Bradford's team of women who visited now in Milton. 'The losses in the Jutland Bank Battle fell terribly hardly on Portsmouth and the shock was appalling,' noted the writer. On the morning of the day on which the news was confirmed, they did indeed visit everyone 'in trouble' in Milton 'and all that could be done was done to bring any possible comfort and relief'. There were fifty-one Jutland casualties from Milton. Issues identified by the visitors were reported to the town hall offices and relief organised. Typical cases dealt with included;

'Mrs C: Ill from shock, special allowance for medicine and nourishing food.

'Mrs H: In distress as she could not afford to continue special arrangements for the education of delicate child. Fees paid.

'Mrs M: Previous delicacy greatly increased by shock. Help over several months given for medical expenses and nourishing food.

'Mrs P: Had had high ambitions for clever boy, help given to continue advanced education.

'Mrs B: Post humus child. Help with expenses of confinement and for nourishing food before and after baby's birth.

'Mrs B: Six children. Children ill with infectious diseases. Help given during illness.

'Mrs R: Delicacy increased by shock. Paralysed child. Nourishing food and medical expenses given. Spinal chair for child to be given.'

'All these and very many other cases of particular trouble need to be constantly befriended,' the writer advised.

Several instances were reported in the papers of men who escaped probable death by being away from their ships at the time. A marine belonging to HMS *Ardent* was home on compassionate leave burying his father. There was a stoker under detention at the Royal Naval Barracks who belonged to one of the cruisers which went down. A telegraphist just prior to the action was transferred from HMS *Queen Mary*, which sank, to HMS *Princess Royal* which was safe. The canteen manager of the *Queen Mary* was sent ashore to attend to supplies and the ship was sent to sea before he returned.

The local papers also reported the return of the first batch of survivors. There were about 100 and they were marched from the town station to the Naval Barracks. They had been kitted out hurriedly in an assortment of ill-fitting clothing and onlookers could be forgiven, in the journalist's view, for thinking that they were new – and raw – recruits, and not the heroic survivors of ships lost at Jutland. At the barracks they were re-equipped and then allowed to depart for their homes. One or two of the men had not been on the list of survivors posted at the Dockyard gates, and the *Portsmouth Times* reported that;

> '…women who had received condolences as widows wept for joy. Among the men saved was CPO Thompson, of the *Invincible*. Thompson's wife had been warned to abandon all hope of seeing her husband again. Friends were condoling with her when the telegram arrived announcing that Thompson was on his way home. Mrs Thompson's experience is rendered the more remarkable since it is the second of the kind which has come to her family. Her sister's husband was officially reported killed, but a month later wrote to the supposed widow, then wearing weeds, from an internment camp.'

Within a week of the news of the Battle of Jutland, came reports of the loss of HMS *Hampshire* and the death of Lord Kitchener on 5 June in the early evening, within only hours of the ship's departure from Scapa Flow for Archangel for a conference with 'our' Russian allies. Only twelve men from HMS *Hampshire* made land alive on rafts. Ten of them were from Portsmouth. Seventy bodies were washed ashore and

Main Gates, Portsmouth Dockyard.   No.615.

Lord Kitchener and his staff board HMS **Hampshire** *at Scapa Flow, Orkney on 5 June, 1916.*

were buried in the Admiralty burial ground at Longhope, 'a picturesquely situated cemetery within sight and sound of the sea.' Lord Kitchener's body was never retrieved. The *Portsmouth Times* quoted a report in the *Aberdeen Journal* describing that night which was one;

'...to make the most experienced seaman quail, as the cruiser steamed across the Pentland Firth, which sometimes has a current

Lord Kitchener on board HMS **Hampshire** *at Scapa shortly before they sailed, 5 June 1916.*

HMS Hampshire, *1914.*

like a mill race, and encountered the full force of the storm from the north-west, leading in from the Atlantic. The sea was literally running mountains high, but the Hampshire made progress till within sight of Marwick Head. Then disaster overtook her.'

Apparently four small boats got away from the sinking ship but there was little hope they would survive the appalling conditions. Next day a passing steamer on passage to Stromness sailed through wreckage. Locals discounted the idea of a torpedo attack in those seas. Even if a submarine could have sailed, it could not have fired a torpedo successfully. Observers on land reported seeing a fire which clearly reached the magazines, and there was an explosion. A survivor spoke in due course to the *Portsmouth Times.* He may well have been William Phillips from St Faith's District who had 'the wonderful escape on a raft' referred to by Garbett in the St Mary's Portsea parish magazine. Whoever it was, he was adamant that the ship did hit a mine at approximately 8.00pm. Talk that she hit a reef was nonsense:

'...as there are sixty fathoms of water there. We went to our fire stations. The Captain called to Lord Kitchener to come onto the fore and aft bridge. I saw him come up with another Army officer – the others also came up separately. I stripped my heavy coat and sea boots off and made for a float (raft). The Captain helped to launch his own boat, but it went to pieces at once. The ship had a great list. No other boat could have lived in that sea.

'The officers and Lord Kitchener walked quietly on deck – they made no fuss at all. I saw one put his hand to his head. They might have been at manoeuvres. No officer left the ship.

'The weather alone caused the loss of life and the ship. We were a mile and a half from shore within easy swimming distance. We considered the Hampshire a lucky ship. We had come through the North Sea action without being hit once, though we were well in it, and near two ships that were sunk.'

Garbett described in the parish magazine 'the dreadful feeling' with which the first news of Jutland was received, and the fear that the navy, 'our wonderful Navy', had suffered a defeat. Happily, he said, those fears were soon dispelled by subsequent reports but nonetheless, Portsmouth was now 'a sad place', and hundreds of homes had been plunged into mourning. A Memorial Service for those who lost their lives in the North Sea and on HMS *Hampshire* was held in St Mary's Portsea on Friday evening 9 June. This church 'has never contained a sadder congregation than that which assembled there on Friday evening', said the report in the *Portsmouth Times.* The building was filled to the doors, 'and there was not a row where someone was not clearly mourning a loved one.' The Bishop of Winchester, Edward Talbot, who had lost his youngest son in the fighting around Ypres twelve months before, preached. He pointed out to the congregation that Portsmouth was bearing three times the burden in death and sorrow that all England bore through her fleet at Trafalgar. Civic and Service representatives included the Mayor, Aldermen and Councillors, the Commander-in-Chief Portsmouth and the General Officer Commanding-in-Chief Southern Command. The music included the Russian Contakion of the Departed, *Give Rest, O Christ, to Thy Servants with Thy Saints* and, at the end, the Dead March from *Saul,* and the hymns *Oh God, our help in ages past* and *Eternal Father, strong to save.* Two days later, on Sunday, Victoria Park in turn was packed with thousands who came to mourn the losses at Jutland and on board HMS *Hampshire* at a well-attended open air service.

The Battle of the Somme began on 1 July 1916. Kitchener's Army was now in place having completed its rudimentary training. It was the greatest volunteer army ever to go into battle. It would be handicapped however by the historic mind-set of its often elderly senior officers from the old peace-time army who were not reconciled to the demands of trench warfare. The Commander-in-Chief, Sir Douglas Haig, believed that an effective barrage would clear a path into enemy territory which an infantry attack would consolidate enabling the cavalry to break through. The attack when it came however was a total failure. The barrage on the first day did not obliterate the Germans. Their machine guns knocked the British over in rows. A total of 19,000 were killed and 57,000 wounded. It was the greatest loss in a single day ever suffered by a British army, and the greatest suffered by any army in the First World War. The experience of the 1st Battalion of the Hampshires – the Regulars – who took part in this initial offensive bore this out. They were on a 20-mile line of attack opposite Beaumont-Hamel, the most formidable of the fortresses on the German line. It had an elaborate system of tunnels and gun emplacements, and stood 200ft above the bottom of the Ancre ravine. It was foul country in which to try and launch the sort of attack which was planned; it was described by Stevens in *The Battle Story of the Hampshire Regiment* as 'a country of swelling ridge and intervening valley.' 'Wave after wave' of troops, he wrote, broke against the 'burrowed rampart' of Beaumont-Hamel.

> 'The Germans on the height brought their trench mortars into action as soon as the British guns lifted, showing that no vital damage had been done by the long and heavy bombardment. Then, through the German barrage and the rake of machine gun fire, the English and Irish troops and Newfoundland Regiment made an immortal attempt to achieve a great victory against all odds.... Some of the leading battalions suffered heavily, for the enemy's gun-fire continued to rake them from the left, the enemy's machine-guns enfiladed them from a village on the right. Nevertheless, battalion after battalion walked out of the wood of death and then going forward at the double... made one of the most glorious charges to the death in history.'

The Times correspondent actually referred to the Hampshires' gallant efforts in his report from the battle front. Some progress was made.

Villages were captured on either side of Beaumont Hamel but they could not be held.

The Hampshires were also deployed, according to Stevens, in the fighting to take the Serre Grandecourt Ridge, another position of great natural strength which had also been heavily fortified above and below ground. As at Beaumont-Hamel, waves of men were sent in one after the other. They lost their much-loved commander in this engagement, and significant numbers of men.

> 'The assault on the ridge contained the most terrific fighting in which the Hampshires had up to then taken part. The Brigadier was killed, and the Hampshires sustained grievous loss in the death of their commander, Lt Col the Honourable Lawrence Palk. The Somersets, the Warwicks, the Seaforths, and East Lancashires also lost their colonels in the great attack. Indeed at its completion, successful though it was, there were only two battalions in the Division intact. Colonel Palk had been in it from the beginning, and was not only a magnificent soldier, but was very dearly loved by every man in the battalion. He had served in the 8th Hussars as a trooper, so keen was he in his younger days for a soldier's life. He had been with the battalion right from Le Cateau to the Somme, and had been in the habit of leading his men to the attack carrying only a walking-stick. The Hampshires' losses in other ranks in this fighting were exceedingly heavy, but according to one writer who came through the bitter ordeal, "Not a man turned back, though it was certain death."'

As for the Portsmouth battalions (the subtleties of which was a *regular* regiment and which a *service* regiment were dropped as war took its appalling toll of the different battalions), the 14th Hampshire (1st Portsmouth) Battalion went into battle on the Somme in early September. They had spent just three weeks in training and 'went over' at dawn. Their objective was the heights above Hamel, a position regarded hitherto as impregnable. They were launched in three waves and met fierce resistance.

> 'Officers paid heavy toll to the enemy's snipers. Few, indeed, reached their objective, for the Huns put up a perfectly murderous fire with machine-guns, and his creeping barrage was a fearful thing.

The Battalion was very badly mauled and was sent back for re-fitting.'

However, they seem soon to have acquired a fearsome reputation for fighting. At Schwaben Redoubt, after a heavy bombardment, they swept through one village to a new objective, and withstood a punishing counter-attack at Thiepval, to the right of Beaumont-Hamel where they were heavily bombed. The episode was reported in the *Hampshire Observer.*

'As soon as they showed themselves they were met with a devastating fire from all kinds of guns, and the nearer they got to their goal the heavier became the rain of machine-gun bullets. Hell is heaven compared to what the Hampshires had to face that day. Yet never a man faltered. Never once did the glorious line of khaki waver. It swept irresistibly onwards, rolled over the enemy parapet, and into their front-line trenches.'

The enemy then brought up reserves and tried to overwhelm the Hampshires with hundreds of machine-guns which swept the captured trench with fire.

'Infantry came up with bombs and liquid fire outfits. Some squirted the fire into the trenches until the Hampshires were moving about in a sea of flame. Others kept raining bombs on the Hampshire lads. Nothing could daunt them, however. They advanced beyond the first line, and charged their foes with the bayonets. The odds were heavily in favour of the Germans in point of numbers, but they weren't the match of the Hampshires for hard fighting; the whole German line was thrown back.'

There were other similar episodes in the trenches when gas, flame and massed machine-gun fire were used to try and repel the Hampshires' onslaught. The attack and counter-attack at Thiepval attracted admiring comment from onlookers, said Stevens.

'"Magnificent!" said a French officer. "My God, you men are fine!" Nothing stopped them; they went through barrages as though they were summer rain. They faced machine-gun fire of an incredible sort without flinching, and in spite of the hammering which they suffered they held every yard which they won…and fought with the casual confidence which became the hall-mark of the Hampshire.'

But no strategic advantage was gained. Haig continued doggedly however to throw men into the offensive until November when the whole enterprise foundered in the mud until the new campaigning season began in spring 1917. Lord Kitchener's Army was destroyed on the Somme and, as many commentators have noted, so was the zest and idealism of the many young British men who had marched enthusiastically off to war. Not surprisingly, back at home, sympathy

Typical popular picture postcard of the day.
(Jordan Collection).

THE GIRL I LEFT BEHIND ME (1).

I'm lonesome since I crossed the hill, and o'er the
  moor and valley,
Such heavy thoughts my mind do fill since parting
  with my Sally;
I seek no more the fine or gay, for each does but
  remind me
How swift the hours did pass away with the girl
  I left behind me.

BAMFORTH (Copyright)

for conscientious objectors was beginning to wear very thin. Their appeals took up a great deal of the Portsmouth tribunals' time as evidence had to be produced of long-held and known objections.

The Portsea clergy were clearly working in the Somme battlefields. The dates on their letters and the general content give that much away but frustratingly there are no detailed addresses. There is not a single letter however, which does not contribute something to our understanding of what it was like for the soldiers in the trenches. The vicious fighting was relieved occasionally by the snatched sight of flowers blooming in the ravaged landscape, the fun of a football match, a delicious dip in a lake on a hot summer's day, and the unexpected discovery of a large farm cat which had adopted a group of men in a dugout. Llewellyn Jones discovered the poppies in the trenches on his way up to the frontline in late July.

> 'My way lay along a piece of ground terribly broken by shell holes and looking the picture of desolation – dug-outs long since abandoned, broken down or fallen in; sand-bags decayed, and many shells, some whole, some fragments. But that passed, a much more congenial way opened up; it was a communication trench, deep and well-drained, beautiful with a profusion of poppies, beautifully red, with long grasses and corn growing with them, and other flowers of various kinds and colours, all adding to the beauty of the way.'

He also took part in an impromptu football match, officers against sergeants, in long grass up to 3ft high with shell holes in places 5 or 6ft deep.

> 'There were no rules to the game, and the work of the referee was only to keep time and blow the whistle when time or half-time came. The game produced much laughter. Many bruises, not a few goals, and at the end of the match some of us were glad that there was a small lake near at hand where we could get a dip, and we were fortunate in having our swim undisturbed by shrapnel or other inconveniences.'

It was a welcome distraction. His next paragraph dealt with 'the grim and deeper side of things.' A glance at the casualty list any day, he suggested, 'will make the smallest imagination grasp something of the

Second anniversary of the outbreak of war, Town Hall, Portsmouth, 4 August 1916.

tremendous sacrifice going on, and press home the need of ever more and more earnest prayers and intercessions.' Such must have been the thoughts uppermost in the hearts and minds of Portsmouth's leaders and people when they gathered in the Town Hall Square on 4 August 1916 to mark the second anniversary of the outbreak of war.

It was J.P. Halet, another Portsea curate, who arrived rather later in France than the others, who reported on the cat which he discovered when he went to lunch with the headquarters of a battalion new to him in a mine dugout, 'which the Boche has taught us to dig into the bowels of the earth.'

> 'The same familiar scene: a table, lit by an acetylene (this is luxury), with the bare necessary utensils on it; four bunks fixed ship-shape to the wall; a collection of stools, chairs and boxes. Seated around the table a Commanding Officer, DSO, an Adjutant, MC, and one or two others, and a cat – a French cat, an ugly cat, a hideous cat; a cat doubtless an aborigine of the ruined village overhead; a cat so spoiled and petted, that its life is one long purr – it will get a sore throat one of these days!'

Edge-Partington's letter to the vicar in early August is an evocative account of his activities when his brigade was called on – and here the looming presence of the censor is in evidence –

'to make an attack on one of those villages which the daily papers tell you we have taken, down by the Somme.' He had no clear idea what he might do to help, 'I simply hoped some opportunity to be useful would turn up.' So he set off to walk the three miles up to the front line. 'After going half a mile across country, I struck a road, which led through a wood and past a cemetery with its rows of little wooden crosses. I next passed a chateau, much battered, which was used nowadays as an advanced dressing station, but today it was too far back. After passing this I came out into the open – may I add, made open by the British artillery. There had been woods, there had been villages within sight, but now hardly a sign of these remained, but instead one looked out upon a bleak, deserted, mangled, torn expanse of country. I had entered those parts over which a British army had advanced.'

He found a road down which he plunged, and soon began to meet wounded members of his brigade coming towards him. He was then hailed from a cart which was moving very slowly in the rear of the column. Half lying and half sitting was the cheery but white face of a sergeant, a keen member of his branch of the Church of England Men's' Society (CEMS). There were other members of the branch amongst the men coming up behind him, again with assorted injuries. They had gone into action at about 6.00am that morning. It was hot and, as he greeted the growing numbers, he decided that he ought to try and organise something for the men to drink. He found a cache of tea in a nearby trench where one of their corporals who had been slightly wounded had been left to await evacuation. The corporal was able to help Edge-Partington make tea, as well as Bovril and cocoa, which was received gratefully. They had run out of supplies by 8.00pm when an officer in charge of a carrying party who was living temporarily in a former German dugout close by, came up and offered him dinner. 'It was A1, a chop and a piece of ration bread and some German soda water.' After dinner, as the evacuation of the wounded was proceeding so slowly, he got hold of a stalwart member of a trench mortar battery, and together they acted as stretcher-bearers. It took them until midnight to carry three cases back to the chateau from where the ambulances picked them up. He stayed at the chateau until 4.00am, helping the doctors, and greeting the men he knew who were brought in. 'On this day I can sincerely say,' he wrote, 'that I realised the value of having been with one brigade since April 1915. These wounded men need a chaplain, but above all they need one they know.'

Llewellyn Jones was awarded the Military Cross for gallantry in attending the wounded and dying in the Battle of the Somme. Garbett announced the news proudly in the Parish Magazine in November 1916. Edge-Partington was similarly decorated in July 1917. St Faith's burst with pride as this award for their parish priest came on top of two Military Medals awarded shortly before to parishioners Charles Piggott and Fred Collis. It also came with the news of Edge-Partington's marriage on 22 February 1917 to Miss Muriel Seymour. They were married early in the morning in the Parish Church when Edge-Partington was home on leave. Garbett officiated. As it was wartime, there was no wedding breakfast and the couple left immediately after the ceremony for a short honeymoon before the groom returned to the Front.

Besides news from the clergy, the parish magazines also report briefly each month on news of parishioners away fighting. There are condolences; information about casualties, those 'missing in action' and prisoners of war; congratulations when Portsea men have been decorated or promoted; and news on who is home on leave or expected home shortly. The report in December 1916 from St Faith's is typical. The author wrote that they had received a good deal of news recently of 'their' men.

'Three of them, alas, are reported missing: Bill Tolliday, George Turner and Charlie Stares. George was the first of our Sunday school teachers to get to the Front, and we were receiving cheerful letters from him until quite recently. Some of his papers and photographs were picked up on the field, but there is no further news of him. Another of our teachers, Wil Wilson, has been causing some anxiety, but we rejoice to hear that he has re-joined his unit after some thrilling adventures. Fred Collis is beating all records in rapid promotion and collecting stripes at a prodigious rate; he is now Company Sergeant Major – and his twenty-second birthday still in the future! Well done, Fred! Two other members of our choir have also been busy putting on stripes viz, George Thomas and Steve Currie.'

The one and only Zeppelin raid on Portsmouth took place on 25 September 1916 at 11.00pm. It was surprising that Portsmouth had not been attacked before given its strategic importance. The first Zeppelin had appeared over the British coast on 29 December 1914, and London was bombed from the air in April 1915. However, the airships were vulnerable to fire from shore-based batteries, and perhaps this risk had been sufficient to deter raiders from visiting Portsmouth before now. Airships were replaced in due course by aeroplanes, and twelve months later four German bombers, flying from their airfield in Belgium, would drop a series of bombs on another dockyard town, Chatham, and the Medway area. One of these bombs dropped on the Drill Hall in Chatham Barracks where 900 men were sleeping or preparing for bed, with devastating results.

The huge lumbering machine over Portsmouth dockyard on 25 September 1916 – like a big, silver cigar, observers reported – was caught in the searchlights at Point battery. It was too high though for the guns of the shore battery to make much impression. This was the noise which awoke local residents and sent them scurrying for shelter. The anti-aircraft fire may have been enough however, to protect the dockyard and drive the airship away from built up areas. It made its laborious way instead up the harbour, dropping four bombs which fell harmlessly into the water. One narrowly missed HMS *Victory,* still at anchor in the harbour, and another the dreadnought HMS *Renown* which was in dock at the time. Only those within hearing of the shore batteries would have been aware of the drama unfolding at the time but it provoked an outcry and frightened people afterwards who feared that this was the beginning of a prolonged series of raids.

Contrary to what the residents may have thought, attack from the air was probably the least of their problems in late 1916. Hit hard, and shaken by the loss of so many of their men during the year, Portsmouth now faced, with the rest of the country, a new and potentially very serious threat to life. Essentially, the country was running out of food. Supplies, particularly grain, had been seriously disrupted by enemy submarines. Political turmoil at the end of the year ended only when Lloyd George, confident that he could prosecute the war more effectively, outmanoeuvred and overthrew Asquith and on 7 December 1916 set up his War Cabinet. He moved swiftly to set up five new departments of state: shipping, labour, food, national service and food production to address the issues of the day. New men – business men with no political experience but proven records in delivering projects – were brought in 'to do a job.' They would, hopefully, replicate the success of the Ministry of Munitions.

Similar enterprise, albeit on a modest scale, was shown now in the establishment here, in Portsmouth, of the Naval Home Industry. Visitors to Milton had become increasingly concerned about what they called 'the cumulative shock' of the appalling losses in their particular area – the daily news of family losses, the constant bereavement to neighbours. In their view the health of children was deteriorating as well as that of their mothers. Doctors recommended 'change of occupation, cheerful surroundings, congenial companionship'. But this was not easy to achieve in wartime. However, with the help of Miss Kelly's team at the town hall, an initiative was developed during 1917 for a Home Industry for Naval War Widows in Portsmouth which would make children's and ladies' clothes by hand, and a range of embroidered items. A light and airy corner property, 101 Winter Road, was purchased, furnished and equipped to provide three workrooms, a showroom, small office and kitchen. The workrooms opened on 8 January 1918 and eight widows and one orphan daughter began work at once. As the enterprise became known, increasing numbers of naval and marine widows and dependents applied for training and employment, and the Home Industry was soon working to capacity with twenty-six full-time workers and eight part-timers working in their own homes.

Orders were taken for knitted coats, jumpers, sweaters and frocks; wraps in silk or wool; children's frocks, overalls and tunics; copies of Old French and English embroideries and chair seats. Boxes of goods were sent on approval or for exhibition. The commander-in-chief's wife took great personal interest in the enterprise and arranged exhibitions of clothes in London and elsewhere to advertise the women's work. Royal patronage was secured for the venture in the 1920s, and a London showroom acquired in Clarges Street, Piccadilly. The organisation was still busily engaged in the early 1930s when it was reported that over 100 women and their dependents had been trained in the Winter Road workrooms, and the quality of the work they produced, particularly the embroidery, was such that they received orders 'from the best London dress establishments.'

The original aim of the project however had been to distract the grieving women living in Milton in 1917, enable them to supplement their incomes and, in some cases, provide them with the means of earning a living. On all three counts, Miss Kelly advised in her first official report in 1918, they had been successful. None of the first recruits were qualified needlewomen and they had made astonishing progress, doing work to which they were quite unaccustomed. She was amazed

> '...to find some of the widows who have been known to me as suffering severely from shock, and to some extent from inertia, working with very evident keenness and enjoyment. One widow in particular who has been considered by us practically unemployable on account of hemiphlegia [a form of paralysis] on the right side, promises to be the best worker of all.'

CHAPTER 5

Seeing it through

Contributions to War Loan – War Savings Committee – Food Shortages – Waste Campaign – Allotments – Allotment Thieves – Food hoarding – Land Army – WAACs – Wrens – Patrolling the Seas – War Pensions Committee – Medical Officer of Health's Reports – Lieutenant R.C.Rundell – Arras – Easter 1917 – Monchy – Paul Nash – Passchendaele – Sergeant James Ockenden VC – Entertaining the Wounded

When the *Portsmouth Times* looked back on 1917 at the end of the year, it commented that since 1914, national life had passed through several distinct and momentous phases, and that 1917 marked the opening of a new period in the direct appeals made now to people, individually and collectively, to help prosecute the war. And indeed, Portsmouth's civilian population did step forward now, inspired by Lloyd George's rhetoric, and led by the borough council, to play a significant role on a new front, the Home Front. Effective systems were in place now to recruit fighting men and manufacture munitions. Fundraising, food production and national service by non-combatants were the issues which became key features of life in Portsmouth in the remaining years of the war.

A War Savings Committee was established and in proportion to its size and population, no town contributed more generously to war loans. Between 1917 and the end of the war, four campaigns raised just over £4,000,000 for the nation's finances, an average of about £20 per head of the local population. The first campaign, for the Victory War Loan, began with a rally in February 1917 in the town hall and the council set a patriotic example by contributing £500,000. The total contribution of the borough came to just over £2,000,000. Of this sum, £85,000 was taken up by small investors. At the end of the year, in December, the second campaign, 'Tank Week', raised £160,000. The Business Men's Week in March 1918 raised £654,000 and the last campaign, in November 1918, 'Feed the Guns', over £1,000,000.

Ingenious schemes were concocted by the War Savings Committee to inveigle money out of the local population. They collected over £3,000 from their own friends to distribute in prizes to those who had War Bonds or Certificates, with numbers drawn from a huge wheel. This was immensely popular and crowds would gather in the Town Hall Square waiting for the wheel to turn and identify the winning numbers. Trenches and a dug-out were constructed from sandbags in the Town Hall Square during the last campaign. On this occasion a decorated 'Victory' tramcar was loaned by the Tramway Committee as well, and the sixpence charged for a ride was used to buy War Savings Certificates for the children in the Royal Seamen and Marines' Orphan Home in St Michael's Road. Regular savers contributed money to War Savings Associations in work places and schools. According to Gates, 233 such organisations were formed with a membership of 27,867, and 328,988 War Savings Certificates were purchased.

In total, during the war the borough council invested almost £700,000 in War Loan which was remarkable because Portsmouth was never a wealthy town. Cleverly, the borough treasurer borrowed the money from the corporation's bankers on the security of the sinking-fund instalments which would normally accrue to the sinking fund during the coming 5 or 6 years. There was no charge on the rates as the dividend received on the war stock was sufficient to pay the bank charges on the amount they advanced.

Food shortages became acute early in 1917 due to the disruption of supplies, and particularly of grain, chiefly due to enemy submarines but also to bad harvests. The local newspapers reported in detail cases of U-boat 'savagery' such as the sinking in January of the British steamer SS *Westminster*, 180 miles from land and *en route* from Italy to Port Said. What outraged the newspaper was the fact that the men attempting to escape the sinking ship were shelled and no attempt was made to pick-up survivors from the water. Early in February, there are reports of twenty-seven ships sunk in two days by U-boats, as their campaign intensified. Garbett referred to 'the real danger of scarcity of food in the country' in his vicar's letter in the March edition of the Parish Magazine. He went on to warn that 'there is not sufficient food for us all to have the full rations of peacetime, so we must all make our sacrifice in this matter.'

The Americans entered the war in April 1917. The U-boat offensive was an attempt to bring this country to its knees before the Americans arrived. By April, one ship out of four leaving British ports did not return. A million tons of shipping was lost, 66 percent of which was British. Neutral ships were refusing to take cargoes destined for British ports. Wheat reserves dwindled to six weeks' supplies. Despite opposition from the Admiralty, Lloyd George insisted that convoys should be introduced. However the very real risk of famine prompted the King's proclamation on 2 May urging strict economy and the avoidance of waste 'in the use of every species of grain.' The borough council rose to the challenge. An Economy Committee was set up in Portsmouth at once to preach economy in foodstuffs, the avoidance of waste and the collection of textile and metal scraps. A Food Control Committee was also established to prevent profiteering and to ensure that orders issued by the Ministry of Food were carried out, maximum prices for milk, meat and coal being fixed.

A scheme was devised with the Education Committee to instruct people on how to prepare cheap meals, and there were public demonstrations in economical cooking. The Portsea Island Gaslight Company in particular organised war economy lectures at its showrooms in Commercial Road on such subjects as 'Home bread baking and bread making with wartime flour.' It was also a good opportunity to extol the virtues, and economy, of gas ovens. The doctrine of food economy was in fact preached so enthusiastically that Portsmouth achieved the proud distinction of creating a record for the country in the reduction of the bread ration to a weekly consumption of 3lb 1oz per head, and secured a promise from the government and the Ministry of Food that exemption would be given from compulsory bread rationing so long as the average consumption remained within the scale laid down by the Food Controller. There was a four week

Waste Campaign in local schools and the children brought in a remarkable 3t of paper, 24,000 bottles, nearly 8t of metal and 15cwt of rags. Food waste was collected from local hotels and restaurants for pig swill and a small committee of ladies was formed to collect waste wool, cotton and paper which could be taken to depots established now in different parts of the borough.

Concurrently with these campaigns, the public were also urged now to grow more food. Food prices had doubled since the beginning of the war and pressure was growing on the council by the end of 1916 to make land available for cultivation. Land belonging to the Board of Guardians, the Borough Asylum and the new hostel for student teachers at Milton was turned over to growing potatoes and other vegetables at the end of November. The Education Committee however resisted for the moment handing over school land. It was also agreed that Victoria Park should not go under the plough as it was the only open space near the Town Hall to which the public had access for rest and recreation.

In the New Year, food production and allotment holding went onto a war footing. The Government established a Department of Food Production under the direction of Sir Arthur Lee who was the MP for the Fareham Division. Power was given now to local authorities to acquire, rent and, if need be, to seize land for conversion into allotments. The Parks Committee secured land in every part of the borough including War Office property, many of their own recreation grounds and several acres on Southsea Common as well as part of Governor's Green. There was keen competition for allotments and the outlying areas of the borough were transformed into useful and productive plots. The general aspect of the borough was transformed, especially on the outskirts, said the *Portsmouth Times.*

Inevitably, the new crops were vulnerable to allotment thieves during the summer months and a case actually came to court in June 1917 to do with the theft of 48 lettuces. The town clerk, Mr F.J. Sparks, prosecuting, asked for exemplary punishment to deter other thieves as there had been a number of complaints of thefts recently. According to the *Portsmouth Times:*

'Mr Sparks said that the punishment for the offence under the Act under which the proceedings were taken was imprisonment (as the alternative to a fine) for a month but if the proceedings had been undertaken under DORA* prisoners would have been liable to 6 months imprisonment and a fine of £100. The Allotments Committee was seriously considering whether in future offences proceedings should not be taken under DORA.'

*D(efence) o(f) the R(ealm) A(ct)

The magistrates took a dim view of the offence and Charles Langford, aged 19, labourer, was given twenty-one days' imprisonment, and Edward Mariner, aged 16, a carter, was fined £1. Costs of one guinea each had to be paid, the alternative being thirteen days' imprisonment.

Cases of food hoarding also came up before the local magistrates. There was a particularly sensational case a few months later in August 1917. Captain Francis Harvey and his wife of Cams Lodge, Hambledon were charged in Portsmouth that they;

'...on divers dates did acquire food so that the quantities of such articles in their possession exceeded the quantity required for ordinary use or consumption in their household or establishment contrary to the Food Hoarding Order of April 1917.'

The house had been searched and eye-wateringly large quantities of food of all descriptions were found stored throughout the property, including the Smoking Room, the Bench was informed. The food included 248lb wheat flour, 140lb barley flour, 14lb maize flour, 11lb rice flour, 12lb oatmeal, 75lb flaked maize, 1lb flaked rice, 7lb wholemeal, 2lb barley kernels, 7lb barley meal, 21lb Quaker Oats, 16lb Provost Oats, 105½lb jam (purchased), 56lb dates, 11lb biscuits, 3 tins biscuits, 64½lb tea, 17½lb rice, 9lb lentils, 5½lb pearl barley, 6 packets cornflour, 2 tins custard powder, 16½lb dried fruit, 103lb sugar, 3 large hams (approximately 80lb), 360 eggs, 15lb raisins, 7lb corned beef, and so the list went on. There was also cheese and, in tins, salmon, ox tongue, butter, margarine, peaches, pears, gooseberries, loganberries, plums, pineapple, raspberries, apricots, marmalade, and potted meats, and packets of soup, beef essence, tea, coffee, cocoa and chocolate. Dried goods included beef suet, split peas and beans, all in enormous quantities. One large box of groceries had not even been unpacked but it was estimated to weigh at least 336lb. The captain and his wife were fined £102 which depending how you do the calculation (real price, labour value or income value) is between £5,000 and £30,000 today.

We can only speculate that the police were tipped off either by the suppliers or by a member of their own household.

A Women's National Service meeting held in the town hall on 27 April launched the campaign to persuade young women to enrol in the Women's Land Army. Originally established in 1915, there was now a determined effort to recruit more young women to help address the current desperate situation. Speakers reminded the meeting that out of every five loaves baked in this country, four were produced using imported wheat. We had beaten the Germans on the battle field but they still had the capacity to starve us into submission. Volunteers would get a free outfit and train fare, maintenance and 18 shillings a week. More details could be obtained at local Post Offices. Portsmouth women signed up enthusiastically. In fact, half the land girls recruited in Hampshire came from Portsmouth, and Hampshire topped the table for recruits from what Gates called the 'provincial counties.' Local girls were sent to work on farms not only in Hampshire and Sussex but throughout the country.

Portsmouth Grammar School also sent boys off to help in the fields. It was reported at prize giving in October that for the first time in the history of the school thirty-two boys, mostly over 16 years-old, put in three weeks work on the land during the summer holidays. They were billeted in the village school at Arreton on the Isle of Wight and during their stay there worked on some fifteen farms within a seven-mile radius.

At the same time concerted efforts began to recruit young women in Portsmouth into the ranks of the Women's Army Auxiliary Corps (WAACs) and the Women's Royal Naval Service (Wrens). WAACs and Wrens were employed initially in a domestic capacity, cooking meals, waiting at table and working in laundries, in barracks and ward rooms across the town, but it was not long before, of necessity, they were recruited to undertake additionally a whole range of clerical and technical duties such as driving ambulances, motor cars and light vans if they were WAACs or working as engineers, electricians, photographers, draughtswomen, tracers and signallers if they were Wrens. The WAACs had a smart khaki coloured coat-frock, greatcoat and cap. The Wrens had blue coat-frocks with sailor collars. Round their caps in gilt letters were the initials WRNS. The Women's Royal

Air Force (WRAF) was originally a section of the Wrens and was formed into a separate force only a few months before the end of the war. However, their presence was limited on Portsea Island as there was only one air-station, at Tipnor.

German U-boats may have been disrupting supplies destined for British ports but the Royal Navy was still successfully blockading the German seaboard. Since the beginning of the war some 26,000 ships had been searched by naval patrols. Many of the naval reservists who mustered in Portsmouth in August 1914 were deployed patrolling and searching in both home waters and further afield. It was hazardous and exhausting work, and went on without remission for the duration of the war. The ships were particularly susceptible to torpedo attack and mines. Lieutenant Vereker (who we left at the end of his time in Portsmouth travelling down to Plymouth on 4 August 1914) was deployed shortly afterwards to HMS *Empress of Britain*, an Armed Merchant Cruiser, which he joined in Liverpool on 18 August. His experiences were typical.

The *Empress of Britain* sailed within days for St Vincent in the Cape Verde Islands where they would get orders on where they were to take up duties as a patrol ship. He was very excited at the prospect. As this patrol was 'in the track of all ships bound home and out to and from England, and all countries for South America and Brazilian ports, we all hope to see a little excitement soon'. In fact he did not report a great deal other than the fact that early in the New Year the captain was sent home 'off his head'. More exciting in the end, and decidedly tougher, were his experiences in the North Sea with the 10th Cruiser Squadron from May 1915. He was the boarding officer and if there was a high-sea running and it was raining, boarding was difficult.

The first steamer he boarded was 'very suspicious'. His captain put an armed guard on board and sent the ship into the nearest British port. The next boat he boarded was a Norwegian steamer bound for Manchester with magnetic iron ore. He spent two hours testing the cargo to see that there was no haematite iron ore mixed with it 'as this is contraband of war.' However, all was correct and the steamer was sent on its way. A Norwegian steam trawler was searched as she had a number of spar buoys out and his captain told him to take them all up and look at them carefully in case the trawler was laying mines. It took him two hours;

> '...as each buoy had about 500ft of line out, all of which were full of small lines with hooks baited with sardines as bait for cod and hake, and also big, hollow glass balls about 40ft apart to keep the small lines off the bottom. I would like to have taken some of the fish but of course wasn't allowed to.'

There was in fact nothing out of order. However, they did send the next ship they searched, the Swedish steamer *Götaland,* into Kirkwall with an armed guard.

Mines were a constant threat. They received advice from one ship they boarded that large quantities of floating German mines had been washed ashore recently on the Norwegian coast. There were also German submarines in the area. Vereker learnt from the skipper of a British steam trawler that he had just sighted a German submarine showing its conning tower. The submarine had clearly sunk a ship as there was a lot of wreckage in the water. Vereker told the skipper and his crew that they should have rammed the submarine. He was delighted however, on this occasion, to be presented with a large basket of fresh herring which was enjoyed hugely that evening for dinner in the wardroom. He was aware though that HMS *Empress of Britain* had a very lucky escape as the ship had passed the position the submarine was in only an hour earlier.

After several months at sea they were sent back to Glasgow. He enjoyed the trip up river 'seeing all the green fields, May trees in flower and glorious rhododendrons after being so long at sea.' It was an all too brief respite however and he was soon back at sea patrolling off the Norwegian coast where the mountains were still covered with snow although it was July, and the sun set at 11.30pm and rose at 1.00am. There was some consolation though in the fact that he had been promoted while on leave to lieutenant commander and first lieutenant, and had proposed, and been accepted, by his girlfriend, Margery.

The tally of ships he boarded in the last months of 1915 grew: Norwegian whalers sent into Kirkwall for examination; an American oil tanker on its way to Copenhagen with petroleum on board, also sent into Kirkwall, and with an armed guard; an American grain ship, again bound for Copenhagen, and sent into Kirkwall with an armed guard and, one day, a large Danish passenger ship, a Norwegian steamer and a Danish steamer, all sent into Kirkwall with armed guards. This particular episode seriously depleted the complement of men on board HMS *Empress of Britain*.

There were rich pickings another day when they boarded a Norwegian steamer bound for Rotterdam from America in early November. The vessel was laden with cotton, rye and other contraband. Her captain would not take responsibility for the navigation of his ship if it was sent into Lerwick so an officer from the *Empress of Britain*, Lieutenant Bennett, and a significant armed guard was put on board. When they returned a few days later, they were able to tell a delighted crew that the Norwegian steamer was 'an excellent prize.' Some 200 cases of rifle ammunition was found in one of the holds and a lot in the chief officer's cabin, and it was reckoned that when the ship was unloaded they would find even more.

Vereker left the 10th Cruiser Squadron in April 1916 and took up a new position in May as boarding officer in the Downs Boarding Flotilla operating out of Ramsgate. The flotilla had to examine every south-bound vessel, to see that they were all in order, and give them instructions on how they were to reach their various ports. His routine was 24 hours out – in a tug – and then 24 hours ashore 'with nothing to do,' he complained. The flotilla boarded several hundred ships a month and by the end of the year, he had supervised the boarding of over 2,000 different vessels. He finished his wartime service commanding HMY *Maid of Honour,* patrolling off St Catherine's Point, Isle of Wight. It was there that they received the message from St Catherine's War Signal Station that the armistice had been signed and hostilities had ceased, and the following day he was recalled to Portsmouth.

By early 1917, charged now to administer the Naval and Military War Pensions Act, the work of Miss Kelly and her team of helpers in the town hall had increased significantly. There had been a name change as well. They were now the War Pensions Committee as their funding came no longer from the National Relief Fund but directly from the government. A report on the committee's work appeared in the local newspapers in the week ending 19 January 1917. They had some 15,000 families on their books. They were notified of all soldiers and sailors discharged and of all grants to be made to these men. They also received information on all Portsmouth casualties, and details of pensions and gratuities payable to widows and dependents. In possession of this information, a team of visitors kept in touch with discharged men, and with widows, orphans and dependents of those who had lost their lives.

They admitted women and children to special homes and institutions. They boarded children out, and made emergency arrangements for the care of children to enable mothers to take a much-needed rest, or to obtain special hospital or other treatments, and in some cases they took entire charge of motherless children and orphans. They also made arrangements for the further treatment of disabled men. Such men might need to go into hospital again. The War Pensions Committee would make the necessary financial arrangements. They would also help men to retrain for civilian life, and worked with the local Labour Exchange to find work opportunities for such individuals.

The Local Tribunal was still meeting regularly to hear applications for temporary or conditional exemption. The job became harder by the week however. Certificates of conditional exemption granted earlier in the war were critically reviewed now and a further 'comb-out,' as it was called, of protected men took place in the course of the year. The tribunal was not unsympathetic. A particular issue was the number of cases coming forward of men in their late thirties running family businesses with only female labour. Another difficult area was the plight of the one-man business if the proprietor was called up for military service. A number of trade associations were summoned to the town hall to discuss the practicalities of forming an association to assist in the conduct of a business if the proprietor was called up.

The borough council was also pro-active in its decision to make provision now for the diagnosis and treatment of venereal diseases, and Portsmouth was the first provincial town in the country to prepare such a scheme. In February, a clinic was established at the Royal Hospital with two RAMC officers appointed as pathologist and medical officer, and in May a publicity campaign was launched at a large public meeting. The town's redoubtable Medical Officer of Health, Dr Mearns Fraser, was confident that the introduction of the clinic would have a marked effect on the health of the town, and indeed the number of cases of syphilis was halved in the first year.

The annual reports to the borough council by Dr Fraser are particularly useful sources of information on the condition of the town in wartime. Overall, he considered that the health of the borough was good throughout the war despite the considerable increase in the number of troops stationed in and around Portsmouth. However, few had been billeted and he believed that it was due to this, and to the fact that the town was 'at all times' a significant naval and military centre, that the increase had had little effect on the general condition of the borough. However, in common with other garrisons, there was a recurring problem with outbreaks of cerebral spinal fever (meningitis) among concentrations of troops living in barrack accommodation. There were thirty-three deaths in 1915 and another forty in 1916. In 1918, there were also 713 deaths in the town from the terrible influenza epidemic.

He was particularly pleased with the returns for 1916 which was a record year;

'...the death rate from pulmonary tuberculosis (consumption) was only 0.95 per 1,000 living, the lowest ever recorded in the borough; only ten deaths from enteric fever were registered – also the lowest ever recorded; only three deaths from scarlet fever – again a record for the borough; and the deaths from diphtheria, 52, were the lowest registered for the past seven years.'

Where there were issues, he addressed them. It was due to his campaigning that the Maternity and Child Welfare Centre was opened in 1915 and the Venereal Diseases Centre in 1916. He was not afraid either to challenge ill-informed assumptions about Portsmouth.

'Some little time back some misguided persons were making wild statements as to the number of illegitimate births that would take place in this town, and calling for special provisions to be made for dealing with the babies. How ill-founded the anticipations were is shown by the fact, that not only has there been no increase in the number of illegitimate births in the Borough but the number registered has actually been the lowest recorded for the past few years.'

Many dockyard workers had brought their families to Portsmouth though, as had a number of soldiers and sailors, and this had placed great pressure on available housing. Never before, according to the Medical Officer of Health, had there been so much over-crowding in the borough, and never have;

> '...the working classes found so much difficulty in finding housing accommodation. Evidence of the difficulty experienced in finding accommodation was afforded by the appearance in the local press of a number of advertisements from persons offering premiums up to a sovereign for houses of a rental of about 7 shillings a week.'

Housing had been a particular concern of his before the war began and he bemoaned the fact that the beginning of hostilities had put on hold the reconstruction scheme for Voller Street in Portsea. He would return to the subject again as soon as the war ended. Nothing was more important he urged, and unless it was dealt with as a matter of urgency 'we cannot hope to retain for Portsmouth, the high position in regard to health which this town undoubtedly occupies at present.'

Despite shortages and queues at home, and the unremitting news of casualties abroad, Portsmouth was still as determined as ever to prosecute the war to a successful conclusion. There was considerable anti-German sentiment expressed at public meetings where the government was urged to intern or repatriate all enemy aliens, and to inflict instant and severe retribution upon Germany for every air raid upon this country's civilian population. The destruction of the Drill Hall at Chatham and the consequent loss of life was an incident which stirred strong emotions in this naval town. The War Aims Committee kept the aims of the allies before the public by means of pamphlets and meetings. In August, an Allied War Photographs Exhibition in the town hall attracted unprecedented interest.

Fortunately the year passed without any heavy British naval casualties, unlike 1916, but in March there was news of the sinking off the Isle of Wight after a collision, of the transport SS *Mendi*. She was carrying 823 members of the 5th Battalion, South African Native Labour Corps to France. The ship had sailed from Cape Town via Lagos to Plymouth before proceeding to Le Havre. At 5.00am on 21 February 1917, the vessel was struck and almost cut in half by the SS

Darro, an empty meat ship bound for Argentina. A total of 616 South African troops (607 of them coloured) and thirty British crewmen died. The sinking of the *Mendi* is regarded as one of the greatest tragedies in the history of South Africa's fighting forces.

The fighting in France continued to take its toll of our forces once the campaigning season resumed. The winter months had been spent in the 'deadly and monotonous' business of trench raids. The Hampshires took part 'winning their due share of death and terrible wounds,' said Stevens. 'Back and fro they went from trench to billets, fighting and resting, resting and fighting, with no more definite change save the occasional home leave.' Lieutenant R.C. Rundell was one of these men. Reg, as he was known, was one of these men. Reg was killed in this war of attrition in the trenches just before the Battle of Arras, the first big battle of the new campaigning season. He was a Portsmouth boy and received his elementary education at Francis Avenue School. He moved on to the boys' secondary school where he became a 'pupil master', and in that capacity attended the Municipal College for two years and obtained an intermediate science degree. He went from there to Reading University where he obtained a Batchelor of Science (BSc). He enlisted on the outbreak of war, and was commissioned as second lieutenant in December 1914 and then promoted to lieutenant in February 1916. He was only 22 years-old when he died. His letters home to his old school friend, Jack, who was working in the dockyard, and keen to volunteer himself, are vivid accounts of this grim period. Advancing across open country was 'a great stunt.' If you made a noise,

'a Bosch plane is sent up. You must stay stock still or drop on your tummy on the ground, in a pool perhaps while a machine gun rakes the ground round you. As soon as plane and gun move on, up you get and continue the race over the empty ground. Very tedious particularly having to navigate the water-filled shell holes. Still once you are wet what does it matter?'

His account of Christmas 1916 is as good as any fictional account:

'Mud! Mud! Mud! We had come up into the forward area on Saturday and taken over a dugout in the centre of a mud waste and near a crossroads (i.e. shells!) "Peace on Earth" had hardly been

France.
Tuesday. 26/12/16.

mud! mud! mud!
we had come up into the forward area on Sat.
and looked over a dugout in the centre of
a mud waste and near a cross-roads (i.e. shells!)
'Peace on Earth' had hardly been fulfilled during
the night 24/25th. for the guns (we were situated
between two lines of batteries) had been
doing 'spasms' all night breaking the rest of
the 'fatigued four' in the dugout. One particular
spasm at 4.30 am. so shook the dugout (it was
evidently a 'Christmas Box') that one of the four
gave vent to a groan, exclaiming,'— + — those
— guns!!" as we other three were duly awake,
we thought it a suitable opportunity to wish
the 'sufferer' a "Happy Xmas" but even that
had far from the desired effect of producing
cheerfulness in the weary one!
Breakfast-time approached, bringing with it
another gift from our gunners of ½ hours duration

Extract from Lieutenant Reg Rundell's 'thank you' letter, 26 December 1914.
(PHC 1002A).

fulfilled during the night 24/25th for the guns (we were situated between two lines of batteries) had been doing 'spasms' all night, breaking the rest of the "Fatigued Four" in the dugout. One particular spasm at 4.30am so shook the dugout (it was evidently a "Christmas Box") that one of the four gave vent to a groan, exclaiming, "____ &____ those____ guns!!"

There was no bacon for breakfast as their rations had been put on the wrong limber coming up the line. They had to make do with bread, and plum and apple jam. Their candles and coal had gone the same way as their rations. It was cold and they were forced to sit in the dark, the only light coming from their cigarette ends. Efforts to sing a few carols fell flat and they passed the rest of the morning recalling memories of past Christmas Days. They cheered up a bit at lunchtime when they ate some preserved meat and vegetable rations. The Germans then began shelling and they sat for four hours 'with a few sheets of corrugated iron between them and 'Promotion to Glory.' Songs died away in the men's shacks nearby 'as those of the birds when a hawk is overhead.'

They then heard someone in waders coming down the steps into their dugout. It was the post corporal with a parcel for Reg. It was the only parcel for their dugout and it was opened hurriedly by the light of matches. Layer upon layer of paper was ripped off to disclose finally 'a huge box of the most perfect chocolates one could wish to see.' There was a chit bearing the words 'To Reg. From Jack.'

> 'Nothing could have been more delightful than to hear from such an old chum in such surroundings. Who cared then if we had no light or the Bosch shelled? Chocolates are easily handled in the dark.... . The ice seemed broken. The Quartermaster Sergeant arrived shortly after with candles and oil rations, and the remainder of the evening was spent in light, harmony, smoking and eating, none could have been happier than the "Four."
>
> Anyway it was the chocolates that "did" it and I'm writing you these few lines to thank you most sincerely for them and your good wishes.'

There is one more letter to Jack, written in February 1917. They are in huts but surrounded by seas of mud as a thaw has set in. He describes vividly scraps in the air above their dugout the previous week.

'It was exciting to see them (they were only about 300ft above us) looping the loop and swerving to catch one another. The Bosch pilot was apparently badly damaged for his plane started settling down, and he limped home, wobbling from side to side pursued by our men and machine guns. He had the luck to just fall in his own lines. Another day one of our chaps came down with a spinning nose dive like a piece of paper.'

Reg was only a name on a piece of paper by the time the offensive began on 9 April to break the German line between Arras and Lens; once again over extremely difficult country. The Battle of Arras was an ill-fated and unsuccessful French initiative in which the two regular battalions of Hampshires fought bravely but for little, if any, gain. According to Stevens, Arras was 'the usual concentration of heavy pieces, the usual bombardment of the Boche emplacements and wire, and then the heart-stirring attack over the mist-ridden, treacherous, and shell-pocked nomansland.'

It was at this stage of the war that the Hampshires acquired the nickname, the 'Tigers', by which they are still known today. Grim accounts survive of hair-raising engagements with the enemy such as the occasion when, as they swept forward, they were caught by the German machine guns and badly mauled but carried on 'again, and yet again', facing the fiercest fire 'with that grim nonchalance which became the mark of the Hampshire men when they were thoroughly 'up against it.' They were 'hosed with machine-gun bullets', and fell 'like grass before the scythe.'

Easter 1917, one of the coldest and most miserable on record, saw the appalling fight for the village of Monchy, 6 miles southeast of Arras. 'No one who served with the 2nd Hampshires during that 1917 Eastertide,' said Stevens, 'will ever forget Monchy, with its scores of dead horses that told of the tragedy of the cavalry who were caught in a snow storm and a shell storm at the same time.' Other historians of these events, quoted by Stevens, confirm what it was like. One wrote that 'the night was dreadful for man and beast. Snow fell heavily, and was blown into deep drifts by wind as cold as ice. Wounded horses fell and died, and men lay in a white bed of snow in an agony of cold while shells burst round them.'

Ellis Edge-Partington was in the midst of these events. He described his experiences in his letter, published, very belatedly, in the July edition of the Parish Magazine. He was asked by an RAMC doctor to set up a collecting place, in a small shelter made of corrugated tin and camouflaged with turf, for the wounded being brought back from the frontline until they could be sent down the line to a clearing station. It was bitterly cold and began to snow. He and an orderly collected wood and made a fire in an effort to keep the stretcher cases warm, hoping desperately that the Germans would not see the smoke or light. He had a flask of rum with which he dosed those who were feeling the cold most. The following morning enough stretcher bearers mustered to take their wounded – some twenty cases now – away.

A few days later, the snow still thick on the ground, he clearly witnessed the cavalry's efforts to storm Monchy, 'the first bit of open warfare which has happened since trench warfare first commenced.' He saw the cavalry charge.

> 'It was a wonderful sight but they were spotted from the beginning, and so in consequence suffered much from heavy shellfire. Owing to the position they found it impossible to get beyond the village, so here they dismounted and helped to hold the line and defend the village from a counter-attack... .'

He spent the day helping to locate the wounded and get them away again. Thereafter the battle 'flared' up and down the line. 'Big shows' followed each other according to Stevens 'at diminishing intervals', and in between there was the bitter fighting which went with efforts to straighten the line. On such an occasion Reg Rundell must have been killed.

Edge-Partington reports regularly when he meets Portsmouth men. Soon after he joined the Army Chaplains' Department he wrote to Garbett that 'Portsmouth can be found anywhere – Good Old Pompey!' It was true. Typical was the occasion he reported now when he met with an unknown bombardier. 'Are you Mr Partington from Portsmouth?' the fellow inquired. 'I go to Kingston Church.' But before Edge-Partington could ask his name, the man ducked back into the trench and was lost to him.

Away from the battle front there were several legendary occasions in 1916 and 1917 when three Hampshire Battalions – the 1st, 2nd and

14th (Portsmouth) – were taken out of the line at the same time, and in approximately the same area. According to Stevens, dinner parties were given in turn by officers in impromptu messes 'and "messes" they often were in that forlorn and desolate land of mud and shells – and the NCO's and men, especially the old campaigners… fraternised freely.' Whether they were regulars or members of one of the service battalions was forgotten. These were brief respites however in what was otherwise a grim and depressing period.

The artist Paul Nash was an officer with the 15th (Portsmouth) Hampshires. He embarked with his draft for France in February 1917, describing them to his wife as a mixture of 'old crusted BEF warriors with wound stripes… and the rest, boys.' They were Portsmouth boys. Like so many, Nash was excited at the prospect of what lay ahead. He and his men were sent to the Ypres sector. It was unusually subdued and, like Llewellyn Jones, he was impressed by the capacity of nature to re-establish itself in the battered countryside. He had not been sent to paint the war at this stage in his career, and he had yet to experience the horrors of the frontline. The illustrations he sent home of scenes comparatively unaffected by war are in stark contrast to those which followed. He was invalided back to England after falling into a trench at night and breaking a rib. He returned to France later in the year as an official war artist, and in the aftermath of the next major offensive.

This was the third battle of Ypres which was launched on 31 July 1917 and would continue until mid-October. Popularly known as Passchendaele, it was an ill-advised venture which in three months floundered barely 4 miles through the Flanders mud in the wettest August in recent memory. The drainage system failed and the men struggled forward on duckboards and, frequently, up to their waists in mud. Guns sank and tanks could not be used. What little gain was made was surrendered in early 1918 when the Germans went on the offensive again. The 14th and 15th Hampshire Battalions, the Portsmouth Battalions which included Nash's men, played their part in these three months of terrible fighting. The 14th took part in a notable engagement in August on the Menin Road when one of their officers, Second Lieutenant Montagu Shadworth Moore, won the VC (the third won by the Hampshire Regiment) for leading his men with conspicuous gallantry over two days, his original force of six officers and 130 men being reduced to just ten individuals. The 14th had an exceptionally difficult time on the Menin Road and also to the south. 'It was desperate work,' said Stevens, 'but it succeeded, and there was a substantial gain of prisoners and of important territory.'

Iillustrations by Nash capture the full horror of this offensive. His angry accounts, contained in letters written to his wife in early November, of what he saw, might equally be descriptions of his own paintings: driving rain, yellow stinking mud, shell holes full of green-white water, black, dying trees, oozing, sweating and rotting tree stumps, broken plank roadways, dead and dying mules and horses, and all the time, whistling overhead and plunging to earth with devastating effect, the shells.

The Battle of Cambrai brought the campaigning 'season' to a close on 20 November when the Tank Corps broke through the German defences in front of Cambrai into open country. The bells were rung in London for the first time since the war began to celebrate this successful offensive but the rejoicing was premature as there were no infantry reserves to exploit the success and ten days later the Germans recovered the lost ground. It was all very depressing. On top of this the Germans had broken through the Italian lines in October and had almost reached Venice, and the Bolsheviks had seized power in Russia, and had promptly signed an armistice. At home an ill-founded panic began over the distribution of food, despite the fact that the country had brought in the best harvest for a century, and there were plentiful supplies generally. Rationing was therefore introduced early in 1918.

However at the beginning of October, Portsmouth was preoccupied with rumours that the 15th (Portsmouth) Hampshire Battalion was likely to lose its name. Following glowing reports from their brigadier general that 'Portsmouth's Own' had worthily upheld the traditions of the town, and that its men were recipients of a long list of awards, the mayor was advised – warned might have been a better word in the circumstances – that casualties had been 'very severe.' Consequently, with the re-manning of ranks came a proposal to change the name to the Hampshire Carabiniers. The mayor was inundated with letters from Portsmouth men at the Front in the Hampshire Regiment appealing to him, and the town, to resist any such efforts. The writers were united in their comments that the battalion had won honours in France, established a good reputation as a fighting unit, 'and that all the Portsmouth lads wish to stick to the old name.' 'They have covered themselves in glory,' wrote one man;

> '...and justified the use of the tiger as their badge by their savage attack and tenacious holding of the line under indescribable fire. Through it all we have borne with us the name of our town, and we have made it a name of which there is no need to be ashamed. Under that name our men have died. We cherish that name... . We have made a name for our regiment, and it is the only fit one. It is sealed with Portsmouth blood.'

Their efforts were in vain. The 15th was amalgamated on 27 September 1917 at Caestre, a small village between Cassel and Bailleul, with the dismounted 1/1st Hampshire Yeomanry and renamed the 15th (Hants Yeomanry) Battalion.

However, Portsmouth did rejoice at the end of the year on the safe return of local hero Sergeant James Ockenden VC, who was born in Alfred Street and educated at St Agatha's School. He received his award for most conspicuous bravery in attack. On 4 October 1917, he was acting as company sergeant major (he was in the Royal Dublin Fusiliers), and seeing that the platoon on the right was held up by an enemy machine gun, he immediately rushed it, regardless of his own personal safety, and captured it. He killed the crew with the exception of one man who made his escape. However, Sergeant Ockenden pursued him and when well in front of the whole line, killed him, and returned to his company. He then led a section to an attack on a farm. Under very heavy fire, he rushed forward and called on the garrison to surrender. As the enemy continued to fire on him, he opened fire, killing four, whereupon the remaining sixteen surrendered.

He was given a hearty welcome by neighbours and friends in Warwick Street where he lived. The street was 'gaily beflagged for the occasion.' He smilingly acknowledged their good wishes, and submitted briefly to the attentions of photographers before escaping indoors with his wife. It may be this occasion which was captured on film by Pathé News. The brief clip shows a tall, good-looking, young man, laughing and smiling, accompanied by a small woman in a close-fitting hat and a coat with a fur collar. However, more likely, it is the occasion when he was presented with his address of congratulation in its 'massive silver casket' at a special meeting of the town council. Or even the occasion when he was introduced to a gathering of Portsmouth's 'Wounded Heroes', some 440, at a reception in the town hall, when he was cheered 'to the rafters' after he had said a few words, modestly suggesting that all of them would have done something similar 'which if it had been noticed by the proper officer would have got him a decoration.'

The town worked very hard to entertain the wounded while they were in local hospitals. The *Portsmouth Times* reported that Portsmouth set an example to the rest of the country. The Wounded Heroes Committee was set up in summer 1916. It raised significant funds each year to entertain the men by organising a sports meeting. The first year made a profit of £450, besides providing entertainment for at least 1,000 wounded. The venture was repeated annually thereafter, and the monies raised were used to provide additional activities. There were weekly entertainments at the town hall and South Parade Pier, and in Victoria Park by professional and amateur artists. Well-known performers, in town to appear at one or other of the local theatres, cheerfully gave their services free. They included personalities such as Vesta Tilley, Lila Field, Irene Vanburgh, Marie Hall and Mark Hambourg. Stars of the Russian Ballet, and famous actors and actresses would also put in guest appearances before commitments later in the day. A number of military bands belonging to such regiment as the Life Guards, the Grenadier Guards and the Coldstream Guards also provided popular entertainment. The Tramway Committee provided free transport to the different venues. Also, there was free access for the wounded to South Parade Pier. The South Parade Pier Committee minutes meticulously note each letter of thanks received for allowing patients from local hospitals free admission to the pier and entertainments.

Members of the Portsmouth Volunteer Ambulance also did a great deal to ease the lot of the wounded. Besides meeting casualties off hospital trains, day and night, at local railway stations, and transporting them to the hospitals, they raised money to purchase non-essential items which contributed significantly to the quality of the men's care such as 'Bath' chairs and easy chairs, sofas, garden furniture,

Fresh air and good company! Probably late 1917 or early 1918.

deckchairs, billiard tables, gramophones, writing materials, and thousands of tram tickets. The bath chairs and their occupants, pushed by volunteer (usually female) labour became familiar sights across the town. Teas were served regularly at the Royal Albert Yacht Club and, according to Gates, thousands enjoyed this particular hospitality. Private motorists also used their own cars and petrol, before its use was restricted, to take parties of wounded men into the countryside for a drive and tea.

CHAPTER 6

The Final Months

Eastern Front – Russian Civil War – HMS Suffolk in Vladivostock – Miss Williams on the Russian Steppes – German Advance in Flanders – Zeebrugge and Ostend – Allied Offensive – Americans in Portsmouth – Rationing – Recycling – Post-war Planning in Portsmouth – Influenza – Armistice – German Fleet surrenders

The final year of the war brought news of local men caught up once again on the Eastern Front, not in the Eastern Mediterranean this time but half-a-world away again, in Vladivostock, on the far eastern seaboard of Russia on the Sea of Japan. Master-at-Arms Herbert Simkins, on board the Portsmouth-built armoured cruiser HMS *Suffolk,* recorded his particular experiences in a diary, including an unexpected meeting with a battalion of the Hampshires in late December 1918.

Allied forces had begun intervening in the Russian Civil War earlier in the year in support of the White Russians, loyal to the Tsar, against the Bolshevik Red Army, in the hope of reviving an Eastern Front against Germany and, long-term, overthrowing the Bolsheviks. HMS *Suffolk* arrived in Vladivostock on 14 January 1918 in sub-zero temperatures, and only with the help of an ice-breaker. Over the next twelve months, the ship protected British interests ashore, providing guards for British residences, including the consulate, and prepared for possible action in a turbulent and deteriorating situation. Simkins describes vividly the dramatic events of 29 June 1918, when all companies on board ship were landed to help the Cossacks. The ship's Maxim guns were put ashore at the same time and positioned on the roof of the consulate where the gunners had a good view of Bolshevik headquarters.

> 'Terrific fire took place during the afternoon, and not until grenades and bombs were thrown did they surrender after suffering terrible casualties, the survivors taken prisoners. The ship's companies returned to the ship about 9.00pm all safe no one wounded.'

Clearly anxious about possible reprisals during the night, as the ship was anchored alongside, *Suffolk's* captain took the precaution of preparing the ship for possible action and loaded the port guns 'but nothing doing,' according to Simkins.

They nursed Cossack casualties wounded in the fighting with the Bolsheviks 'up country' on board *Suffolk*, and during August watched the large numbers of British, French, Japanese and American troops arriving to be sent to the new front. They sent up guns from the ship to the frontline. However, even here they were not immune to the influenza epidemic. During one week in October, 105 men were on the sick list with influenza. There was an occasional diversion in the form of a duck-shooting party for the officers and they were still there when, finally, on 12 November 1918, they received a telegram informing them that hostilities had ceased at 5.00am the previous day. There was great rejoicing, and amongst the jollifications organized was a march-past by newly-arrived men of the 1/9th Hampshires and the band from HMS *Suffolk*. A few days later, the Hampshires also gave a concert which the crew of *Suffolk* decided was 'very good.' The 1/9th Hampshires had begun life as a Territorial Battalion (Cyclist) in Southampton in 1914 but were joined with three other cyclist battalions and converted to infantry in 1915. They were sent to India the following year and in October 1918 were among the British troops sent to Vladivostock. Soon after, they were moved on to Siberia and would not return to England until the end of 1919.

Also in Russia, at the Angliskaya Mission, Buzuluk in Samara Government, on the edge of the Asiatic steppes in Eastern Russia, was Miss Theodora Williams from St Wilfrid's Mission, George Street, Portsmouth, another of the Portsea Mission Churches. Her letters home, published like the clergy's letters in the Parish Magazine, throw light on a seldom reported subject – the flight and plight of enormous numbers of refugees from the various Russian provinces in the war zone. After suffering appalling hardship the refugees were relocated to other 'governments', as the Russians usually called their provinces, far afield from their original homes. Penniless and starving, they were quartered on the local population who accepted them into their homes despite having precious little themselves. Many of the male refugees had been diverted into fighting or other war work so did not need help but their women folk did. Miss Williams described what she did. She was in charge of a workroom at the mission where women pulled, sorted and cleaned wool, and then wove it into cloth or spun it for stockings; they also knitted and sewed. She was pleased to report, as Miss Kelly discovered in Milton, that many of the women cheered up considerably once they had something useful to do for which they were paid.

She described the scene from her windows, which she knew would delight the Portsea children, a long train of camels each drawing a rough little cart, coming slowly over the steppe. Apparently camels were greatly used, and very hardy. In winter, often covered with white frost, they drew sledges through the deep snow. She described the vast level steppes stretching far away to the horizon, like a great flat, green sea dotted here and there with little mud villages of 'incredible' poverty but always with a beautiful, white church topped with a silver or golden dome. In every house was an icon with a lamp in front of it 'and no Russian thought of entering a house without first doing reverence to it; and every tiny child crossed itself and bowed to the icon before and after eating, even before taking medicine!'

In addition to her duties in the workroom, she also worked in the hospital. Nearly all the Russian doctors had gone to the Front leaving huge districts without any medical provision whatsoever. Their unit of three doctors, eight nurses, and two orderlies had charge of a district larger than Belgium, containing hundreds of villages.

'But we have one hospital in our centre, out-patients' departments in four, and in two a district nurse and little dispensary. I wish you could see our crowded out-patients' departments. All sorts of people come – Khirgeez or Khirghiz (don't know how to spell it), Tartars, Cossacks, Tuwashes, and other semi-Asiatic folk, as well as the

Russian peasants, and the languages are as varied as the costumes, and that is saying a good deal.'

Theodora Williams describes a world as far removed from the lives of her readers in Portsmouth as the stories from *Tales of the Arabian Nights*. A person risked being killed in the war but it did give many people unexpected opportunities to see the world which would never normally have come their way. Ernest Bruce's experiences are a case in point. Between detailing the fighting in Palestine, in which he was engaged on the outskirts of Jerusalem, and expressing his anxiety about how his sisters and his parents were coping running the family business, he describes some of the local sights. 'Ern', as he was known by his family, was the only son of dairyman James Bruce of Highland Road, Eastney. He was in the Lancashire Regiment, and his family was associated for many years with Eastney Methodist Church. Shortly before he was killed he wrote to his sister, 'Well Ada, I have seen the Hill of Temptation that is the Place where Christ was tempted forty days and nights all around the top is a stone wall and at the side is a place of worship. I have also seen the Virgin Mary's Tomb and the Garden there are many more places of note what I will try and tell you if I have the luck to come home.'

He speculated in the same letter about whether 'Curly', the family dog, would even recognise him now, as he had been away for so long. He never found out, and Ada did not receive any more accounts of the sights in the Holy Land. His luck ran out. Ernest was killed in May 1918 and is buried in the Jerusalem Commonwealth War Graves Cemetery.

The different battalions of the Hampshire Regiment served on every frontline across the world: on the Western Front in France and Belgium, on the Gallipoli Peninsula in the Eastern Mediterranean, in Egypt, Palestine, India, Mesopotamia, Persia, Salonika and Russia. There are a few good accounts of what troops saw when they were on the move. Edge-Partington and several of his fellow Portsea clergy describe lengthy and uncomfortable train journeys, and cramped troop transports, on the way to the frontline. Other writers describe troop trains taking days to cross the interminable Russian landscape, the flat horizon relieved only by railway halts and oil derricks.

There is a good account of his travels by Able Seaman Gunner Frank

Greenwood who was awarded the DSM for action in Flanders in 1917 with the Naval Brigade. He volunteered for overseas service in June 1918 and was drafted to HMS *M33* (Monitor) in the Eastern Mediterranean. For the best part of September 1918, he and the rest of the draft crossed Europe at a pace more reminiscent of an eighteenth century Englishman on the 'Grand Tour', and expressing not dissimilar sentiments. The expedition began in Cherbourg at a rest camp in an American YMCA where you could write letters, he reported, and where they were entertained by four French ladies with music and songs 'which were very much appreciated.' They then travelled the length of France by train. Passing into Italy, they noted that 'the country so far is rather hilly.' They crossed Italy, left some of their party in the port of Ancona, and travelled down the Adriatic coast which was pronounced 'very pretty, much like the scenery around Teignmouth and Dawlish.' At Bari an idyllic weekend seems to have been spent swimming, writing letters, sun bathing and, to their delight, watching moving pictures – 'movies' – on the beach before they embarked on a ship which would take them through the Corinth canal and their rendezvous with *M33*. Of this last leg of the trip, Greenwood wrote 'lovely scenery steaming between small islands, the sea is like a mill pond. We see a lot of porpoises swimming alongside the ship and flying fish also.' They had been sent to support the allied force on the Salonika front, but by the time they arrived the offensive on the Western Front in September 1918 had already resulted in the capitulation of Bulgaria and the liberation of Serbia. While they waited for further instructions, news of the armistice was received on 11 November, Greenwood wrote;

> 'Great rejoicings. At Stavros and Salonika (spliced the main brace) or gave the men an extra tot of rum. Guns were fired, sirens blown, Rockets and very lights were fired at night and Bells were rung. Leave was given on shore.... Our captain (Commander Patch) gave each man of his ship's company a bottle of beer to celebrate the day when hostilities ceased. We had a very nice sing song after supper.'

There was no let up for the Hampshires on the Western Front in the final year of the war. It was intensive fighting all the way, costly in terms of lives, onerous, and exhausting. The German breakthrough (21 to 28 March 1918) on the old Somme battlefields, when they advanced some 40 miles, took an appalling toll of the Hampshire battalions. They regrouped however and 'went forward with the flood,' to use F.E. Stevens' phrase, 'and like a flood they took part to the final crushing of the enemy.' Sometimes they made 5½ miles in a day. On other occasions they were forced to pull back under heavy fire. They were caught up in particularly grim fighting in marshy and difficult country towards the end of April. It was an anxious time for those waiting for news in Portsmouth.

Garbett's monthly letters echo these anxieties while at the same time providing a useful commentary on events at home and abroad. His April letter urged everyone to stand firm as the German offensive got under way. 'We may have to fall back', he said, but our cause is right and he derided those who argued that peace might be advantageously negotiated with the enemy. The next month he conceded that the situation did give grave cause for anxiety. Many guns had been captured and men taken prisoner but he urged his readers not to be despondent. The Germans could not possibly sustain this momentum, and every week meant increasing reinforcements from the United States. They could be consoled as well by the news of the daring naval raids on Zeebrugge and Ostend on St George's Day. Sadly, he had to report that former choir member, Will Ogden, had been badly wounded in the recent fighting and had died in hospital in Rouen. There was also a growing list of casualties from St Faith's.

More of the staff left the parish in June, two to serve as chaplains and the third for work in the YMCA or Church Army huts. With only six of his original team of sixteen staff left, Garbett announced that he would have to re-arrange the work of the parish. He would keep the mission churches open, but only if the laity were prepared to take a more active part in their activities. By July, along with news of who had been decorated, wounded or taken prisoner, he was writing that the conflict was 'Armageddon, indeed!' He urged the parish to pray. Their prayers were answered! The allied offensive began in front of Amiens on 8 August 1918, when 456 tanks went forward in mass formation. The success was almost as great as at Cambrai but, once again, the Allies did not have enough infantry to follow up and the attack stopped before another too unwieldy a salient was exposed.

The wrecks of HMS Intrepid *(left) and HMS* Iphigenia *allowed only a narrow channel to be navigated at low water. The remains of HMS* Thetis *is in the distance.*

However, another attack began, at a second point, where German reserves had been withdrawn to stem the first Allied advance. The Germans were forced to fall back in one place after another and in due course withdraw their entire line.

Garbett's response was cautious. There was much to cheer us up though. The attack on Italy had been repulsed as well as the latest attack on the Western Front. The French had counterattacked magnificently and the American presence on the battlefield was increasing rapidly. The threat from U-boat attacks also seemed to be receding and there was evidence of growing anxiety and discontent in Germany. By September, he had thrown caution to the winds:

> 'August has been a wonderful month. Early in July we were anxiously waiting the German attack. It had been advertised with the utmost confidence as the knock-out blow, which would secure Prussian supremacy. The Allies were convinced that they could prevent their foes from securing their aim, but few of us dared to hope for an offensive this year; at the best we anticipated a successful defensive. And now, day after day the papers record new victories. The Germans are rapidly withdrawing, leaving behind numbers of prisoners and vast quantities of munitions. At the moment of writing it is impossible to say how far we shall be able to continue this advance, but there is no doubt it brings us appreciably nearer victory and peace.'

He wrote his letter for the November magazine in October 1918. He

An aerial reconnaissance photograph of the harbour entrance after Operation 'ZO', the attack on Zeebrugge.

did not know then that the armistice would be signed early the following month. He reported happily that the greater part of Northern France had been liberated; also Ostend, Bruges, and the Belgian coast. Bulgaria had surrendered long ago and Turkey had now followed. Austro-Hungary was rapidly disintegrating and clamouring for an armistice, and he anticipated Germany asking for terms imminently. 'But this is still only a possibility.' It was in his December letter that he recorded finally the news that they had been hoping and praying for, and he would remind his readers that 520 members of the parish had died in the conflict.

The news of the raids on Zeebrugge and Ostend on 23 April was received rapturously in Portsmouth. 'No more daring deed is recorded,' cried the *Portsmouth Times,* 'than the brilliant raid on Zeebrugge and Ostend which was carried out by our naval forces on St George's Day when two obsolete British cruisers laden with concrete were sunk at the entrance to the Bruges Canal.' A submarine also rammed the viaduct linking the shore and the mole to isolate the German garrison.

In a diversionary move, storming parties of marines landed on the mole to divert the enemy, and gallantly engaged the defenders in a fierce fight which cost the British side dearly in terms of casualties. The raid was an attempt to block the Belgian port, a base for U-boats and light shipping, and thus prevent the Germans leaving port. Ostend was another U-boat base. Two more blockships laden with concrete were run ashore there and blown up. Airmen reported that the greater part of the channel at Ostend was blocked, and that there was a clear break in the mole at Zeebrugge. Neither raid achieved precisely what had been intended nor was the canal closed for long. In fact it was opened only a few days later to submarines operating at high tide. The British also suffered serious losses; a total of 583 men were killed. The Germans lost only twenty-four men. However, the sheer effrontery of the raid captured people's imagination at a time when the country needed some encouraging news and the event was celebrated as a great victory.

There were local casualties amongst the men killed including a number of marines. One officer and seventeen NCO's and men from Eastney were killed, and thirty-nine men died who came from Gosport, including their colonel who was killed in the landing on the mole at Zeebrugge. They were buried either in Anns Hill Cemetery in Gosport or Kingston Cemetery in Portsmouth. The reception given to the survivors when they returned to their depots was memorable. Two men received the VC, and nine petty officers and men received the DSM for conspicuous gallantry. There was also a posthumous award of a DSO to an engineer-lieutenant. His widow received his award. Two Liverpool steam ferries, HMS *Iris II* and HMS *Daffodil,* which played a conspicuous part in the attack on the mole, paid a visit to Portsmouth before returning to the Mersey. They were visited by 12,000 people and £286 was raised for naval charities.

The drama of the Zeebrugge raid was a rare beam of light in an otherwise depressing spring. Like Garbett's letters to his parishioners, the news in the local papers reflects this. There are more reports of the 'invaluable work' of the volunteer ambulance workers, meeting convoys of wounded now at the town station, and conveying them to military hospitals in Portsmouth and the surrounding area. They had received seven new motor ambulances which had been presented to them in February. The donors included Sir John Brickwood; rival brewer, and owner of Portsmouth United Breweries, Colonel Sir William Dupree; Southsea department store Knight & Lee, and Mr and Mrs Ray of Bembridge Crescent, Southsea, who presented one in memory of their son, Lieutenant Eric Ray RN, and the officers and men of HMS *Queen Mary* who died at Jutland.

The pressure on hospital places for the wounded was so great that the Board of Guardians now gave up the greater part of their Infirmary to military patients by handing over three additional wards in April so making provision for 700 men. Shortly afterwards, the Asylum Committee handed over the borough asylum to the Americans who established Base Hospital No.33 there. The asylum patients were moved to other institutions within a 60-mile radius of Portsmouth. Within a very short period the asylum buildings in Locksway Road were converted into a well-equipped hospital with accommodation for 1,500 patients and, in specially built huts in the hospital grounds, space for another 2,000 men. The first convoy of casualties arrived in late July and within 14 days, there were 500 patients.

Valiant efforts went into making the visitors welcome. Sir William Dupree was credited with launching efforts by inviting all the American airmen in the district to a fete in the gardens of 'Craneswater', Southsea. Other events were organized. There were more garden parties, tea parties, trips into the surrounding countryside, even games of baseball against local teams. A hospitality scheme was also devised with the assistance of the Rotary Club, and a committee set up by Alderman Harold Pink, to welcome the American visitors into local homes. A local branch of the American YMCA was established in the town under the direction of Dr Amos Burr, DD. A soldiers' hostel was established in the centre of town at the corner of Hyde Park Road and Waltham Street. The American Red Cross attached several officers to the hostel who organized appropriate facilities and a programme of entertainment. After the war ended, the team there was also called on to organize the passage back to the United States of local brides who had married some of the troops!

In the meantime, the Home Front soldiered on stoically. There was great pressure to supply more allotments. In early January, a representative of the Food Production Department of the Board of

Agriculture, Mr Scroggs, paid a visit to Portsmouth. He congratulated the town on the keenness and enthusiasm of its allotment holders 'particularly in clearing the most unlikely pieces of ground and placing the same in a state of cultivation.' He hoped to see another 50 acres of land brought under cultivation shortly at Great Salterns. The demand for 'your own' small plot of land was understandable. In early 1918, there were serious shortages of meat, butter and margarine, and other essential foodstuffs which lead to frustrating waits in long queues, sometimes numbering up to several hundred women and children, with no guarantee that when your turn came, there would be any of the precious commodities left to buy. The introduction of rationing and ration books, masterminded by the newly-established Food Control Committee at the town hall, at least ensured that there was equitable distribution of available supplies.

Ingenious recycling activities were reported in the local papers. The corporation's Scavenging Department was actually making money. In addition to de-tinning apparatus, it had erected plant for the extraction of fat from hotel, camp or household swill; the edible waste being separated from that going to the destructor, and the residue being used for pig food in the municipal piggeries established at Baffins. Fruit stones and nut shells were also being collected for use in gas-mask filters. In addition, council committees gave serious consideration to the question of establishing communal kitchens. They did not proceed with the idea however as it was felt that local conditions did not really warrant this sort of intervention.

There are also reports in the newspapers which indicate that the borough council was beginning now to think about life in the town after the war. Although the Admiralty moved very swiftly to stop rumours of cutbacks to naval work when the war ended, real fear remained and the council resolved, in February 1918, to revisit a scheme which had been discussed in the past and then commission a feasibility study on developing Langstone Harbour for commercial shipping as part of a wider scheme to diversify the local economy. They also secured a two-year option on purchasing 540 acres of land on the southern slopes of Portsdown Hill for housing.

The Prisoners of War Committee continued to organise social events for PoW's families and send much-needed parcels of food and other necessaries to the men languishing in prison camps in Germany. The different War Work Depots were still busily engaged providing hospital supplies and comforts for troops at home and abroad. In a new departure, they were having some success interesting men in local hospitals to do handicrafts. In December 1917, a sale of needlework by wounded servicemen, who had been instructed by a volunteer group of ladies, was organised in the town hall. Visitors were astounded by the quality of the work. Local people answered the call in June for volunteers for three months' service to improve the defences on the East Coast thus enabling younger, trained men to be released for service overseas at this critical stage. The War Pensions Committee turned its attention to providing training schemes for disabled men discharged from the services. It was no mean task. By October 1918, there were 4,365 disabled men on the Portsmouth Register according to a report submitted to the committee at its quarterly meeting by the Disablement Sub-Committee. Courses were delivered by the Municipal College and began in September 1917, initially for electrical engineering and later, for motor vehicle mechanics. In due course, boot and shoe making and repair were added and later, commercial skills. Many of the men were successfully employed, eventually, in the dockyard and a range of local firms. Not unlinked was the announcement that a new orthopaedic centre would be built shortly at the Alexandra Military Hospital where it was hoped that a limb-fitting centre would be established once the new building was complete.

The vicar of Portsea succumbed to the terrible influenza epidemic in the autumn. Garbett claimed to have had 'flu twice and, for the first time since he was ordained, had taken to his bed and been forced to cancel engagements. In early October, the schools in the town were closed as 177 teachers and 45 percent of the school children were absent. It was hoped that by closing all schools for a week 'the symptoms of illness would have passed away,' according to the *Portsmouth Times*. Dr Mearns Fraser, the Medical Officer of Health, reported that influenza with pneumonia claimed the lives of 713 local people.

On 11 November 1918, there were memorable scenes in Portsmouth when news of the armistice came through. The Commander-in-Chief, Sir Stanley Colville, heard the news first, and at 7.00am in the morning, only two hours after the armistice had been signed, the Mayor, Councillor John Timpson, was told. A tremendous shout went up from the parade ground at the Royal Naval Barracks shortly before 9.00am, and over 1½ hours before the official news came through from the press bureau. The 'General Assembly' was sounded by the barracks buglers at 8.40am and all officers and men, including the Wrens, fell in on the parade ground in double-quick time. Rear Admiral Pelly announced the good news, that an armistice had been signed:

> 'Officers and men, and others, I think this is not only an occasion for three cheers but for a yell. Now yell!" And yell they did, until they were hoarse. The Union Jack was broken as the National Anthem was sung, and a victory psalm and prayer were afterwards recited. Further cheers were given, and finally the Band played "Land of Hope and Glory.'

The news spread like wild fire through the town. The bells at the workhouse and at Kingston Prison rang out, workmen downed their tools in the dockyard to cheer and people poured onto the streets. A special edition of the *Evening News* was published, but the printing machines could not keep pace with demand. The Town Hall Square and adjacent streets were thronged with soldiers, sailors and townsfolk. All vantage points were seized including the statue of Queen Victoria and the lions on the steps of the town hall. The mayor mounted a table and made the official announcement that the armistice had been signed this morning and that hostilities had ceased. He called for three cheers for the army and navy. There was a resounding response and at the same time the sirens of vessels in the harbour, works hooters and church bells broke out in the most amazing uproar. Overhead the 'Pompey Chimes' rang out in celebration from the top of the town hall for the first time since war was declared. There then followed a short religious service led by Dr Amos Burr from the American YMCA hostel, the Reverend W.H. David, Vicar of Portsmouth and Mr Walter Ward, President of the Free Church Council. Garbett gave the blessing at the end of the service.

Most places of business closed for the day, school children were given a holiday and servicemen were given general leave from noon. Processions of sailors and soldiers rolled up and down Commercial

Armistice Day, Town Hall Square, 11 November, 1918. **(Gates, Records 1835-1927).**

Road arm-in-arm with WAACs and Wrens. Tramcars and private road vehicles were decorated and at nightfall, fireworks, rockets and coloured lights lit up the sky. Places of entertainment were packed, and thanksgiving services took place in all the local churches. However, at sea, ships were told not to relax their vigilance immediately as it was possible that German submarines on patrol might not know yet that the war was over.

The surrender of the German fleet ten days later on 21 November 1918 was an event which resonated particularly in Portsmouth. Chief Petty Officer Edwin Fletcher, a Southsea man, was present that day on an unspecified battlecruiser in the Firth of Forth and described the historic events which took place in his diary which he had painstakingly kept since his first days as a rating. He noted that the German cruiser SMS *Konigsburg* with German Government representatives on board arrived and anchored off Inchkeith in the Firth of Forth on 15 November. A conference took place the following day on board HMS *Queen Elizabeth* 'with reference to the bringing over and surrendering of the German Fleet.' Fletcher described what happened on 21 November;

'All Grand Fleet and destroyers put to sea at 4am and rendezvous about 50 miles SE of May Island. Sight German Fleet of nine Dreadnoughts and five battle cruisers which are surrendering by terms of the armistice. 'Our' fleet formed two columns one each side of the German Fleet, also two of our airships and an aeroplane at 9.30am. They are the pick of their fleet, two more ships have got to come yet we were at Action Stations all the time. When we were off Inchkeith the *Queen Elizabeth* with Admiral Beatty on board stopped engines and as our Fleet passed him each ship gave him a good cheer as she passed. Our squadron anchored off Rosyth by 2pm. Remainder of the Grand Fleet with the German Fleet anchored in Burnt Island Roads. With our fleet we've a squadron of American Battleships one French cruiser and two destroyers. Admiral Beatty signalled to the German Admiral Van Reuter to haul the German flag down at sunset, and not to hoist it again without permission. By the Germans surrendering their capitol ships brings the war practically to a close.'

Lieutenant James Colvill's account of what he saw is more detailed. He was on board and in command of the destroyer HMS *Rocket*. Like Fletcher, he wrote that the surrender took 'a deal of discussion' and, again like Fletcher, confirms that there was anxiety about the possibility of retaliatory action:

> 'Many of us thought that they would have a last scrap just to save their sea faring honour (or what little of it was left). It seemed incredible that a service of proved courage should tamely hand over a powerful fleet without show of resistance.'

He described vividly the arrival of the German destroyers in five columns, ten ships in each, keeping excellent station. Their flotillas turned and took up station on both flanks ahead and astern of them. All told there were 172 destroyers manoeuvring together, fifty Germans surrounded by 122 British. They made up twelve columns. In this formation they steamed very slowly up the Firth, and anchored off Leith mid-afternoon. There the work of searching the German ships began.

> 'My luck held and one of the biggest boats fell to me. Her captain seemed a very decent sort of Hun with Iron Cross complete. He spoke excellent English though we were on most formal terms. It was an interesting but rather unpleasant job.'

Unpleasant it might have been but, as Fletcher said in his concluding remarks, by surrendering their High Seas Fleet the Germans effectively brought the war to a close.

CHAPTER 7

Epilogue

Victory Celebrations and War Memorials - HMS Centurion

The year 1918 ended in a whirl of victory parades, pageants and balls. Supplies of oranges, nuts, figs and dates actually arrived in the town on Christmas Eve. Some 750t of coal was released from stocks which had been held in case of emergencies to ensure that no one went without a fire over Christmas. Pork meat and pork sausages could be obtained now without coupons and restrictions were lifted on the manufacture of crumpets, muffins, tea cakes and 'light pastries.' The weekly sugar ration per head was increased from 8 to 12 ounces, and the fighting men and the prisoners of war began coming home. Pious hopes were expressed at church services and public meetings that out of the recent carnage a new world order might emerge governed by law and not violence and, here at home, in Garbett's words, that the energy used to fight the enemy might be used now to combat 'poverty, wretchedness and squalor.'

When the actual peace treaty was signed at Versailles, near Paris on Saturday, 28 June 1919, the navy fired a 101-gun salute and the local population, according to Gates in *Records of the Corporation,* 'let themselves go.' The following day 40,000 people were sufficiently sober to attend the thanksgiving service held in the Town Hall Square. Official celebrations took place a few weeks later on 19 July 1919. There was a grand pageant which wound its way round the town and a banquet in the evening in the town hall. A garden party took place in Victoria Park for the men who had served and in the evening there was

German U-boats in Portsmouth Harbour, late 1918 or early 1919.

a torchlight tattoo. The German U-boats brought into harbour in due course, attracted hundreds of sightseers.

How best to commemorate the dead occupied the minds of many people in the immediate post-war period. Garbett and St Mary's Church resolved to erect a large stone cross in the churchyard, and convert the

Royal Naval Barracks illuminated, Peace Night celebrations, 19 July 1919.
Jordan Collection.

Town Hall Square, Peace Night celebrations, 19 July 1919.

War Chapel into a permanent Memorial Chapel; St Paul's, Southsea proposed completing the Long Memorial Hall by the addition of an up-to-date infants' school; St Luke's was erecting a parish institute and St Bartholomew's, Southsea considering several plans for the 'beautifying' of the interior. It was hoped that none of these schemes would be as critically received as the Parish Calvary and War Shrine, which had been erected by St Matthew's, Southsea the previous year in memory of the men of the parish who had given up their lives. Mr J.A. Kensit, son of the Protestant agitator, John Kensit, had denounced the revival of wayside shrines generally as part of a movement to introduce 'Romanism' into the English church. Less contentiously, a roll of honour was being kept in every parish and, most importantly, plans were in hand for an impressive Town Memorial. Built to the designs of J.S. Gibson and W.S.A. Gordon, it cost £100,000 and was paid for by public subscription. It was unveiled by the Duke of Connaught in 1921. The memorial, adjacent to the Town Hall and

The Town War Memorial shortly after it was unveiled in 1922.

The War Memorial today.

War Memorial dedication plaque today.

A detail on the War Memorial depicting a Lewis gunner.

A detail on the War Memorial depicting a Vickers machine-gunner.

Victoria Park, is in in the form of a circular-walled enclosure with classical archways and has a tall cenotaph.

There are two memorials to the Wyllie boys killed in the war in Portsmouth Cathedral. Billie is commemorated in a fine bronze. He was killed in action at Montauban, on the Somme, on 19 July 1916 whilst acting as brigade major and is buried in Mametz Cemetery. He left a widow and three children. Bobbie is commemorated in a painting by his father of Jesus beside the Sea of Galilee calling Peter and his companions to join him as his disciples. Local tradition has it that the faces of Jesus, Peter and the other fishermen were neighbours and friends of the Wyllie family, living near them on Point. Bobbie was in 'H' Company, 1st Battalion London Scottish. He fell at Messines, near Ypres, on 31 October 1914. Messines was a stronghold valued not only

Memorial to William (Billie) Wyllie in Portsmouth Cathedral.

for its strategic position overlooking the plain but for the extensive system of cellars under the convent known as the Institution Royale. It was taken from the British by the Germans 31 October - 1 November 1914.

The people of Orkney erected an impressive square, stone tower – the Kitchener Memorial – at the top of Marwick Cliffs on the western end of mainland Orkney. The tower is dedicated to the memory of Lord Kitchener, and to the officers and men of HMS *Hampshire*. It looks out over the waters where the ship sank and, in the words of the inscription, stands 'on that corner of his country which he had served so faithfully nearest to that place where he died on duty.'

The Royal Naval War Memorial designed by Sir Robert Lorimer stands in a spectacular position on Southsea seashore, on the edge of the deep-water channel which brings every ship into and out of Portsmouth Harbour. It is a tall tapering column which ends in a finial with a globe. Corner projections are surmounted with stone lions. It was unveiled in 1924. The inscription carved on one of the panels reads as follows:

'In honour of the Navy and to the abiding memory of those Ranks and Ratings of this Port who laid down their lives in the defence of the Empire and have no other grave than the sea, 1914-1918.'

Memorial to Robert ('Bobbie') Wyllie in Portsmouth Cathedral today.

A register of the actions in which the men took part and of the ships engaged was issued by the Admiralty. The number of names upon this part of the Naval Memorial (it was extended by Sir Edward Maufe in 1955 to commemorate the Second World War) is 9,279. The introduction to the register concludes with the following tribute:

'Each entry in these Registers represents untimely death and the bereavement of a family. Together they represent the price paid by those families and the Empire for keeping our shore inviolate; for moving here and there, as we would, greater Armies than the Empire had ever before dreamed of raising; for confining to its harbours, during almost the whole of four years, the greatest Navy except our own; for annihilating enemy sea-borne trade; and for a decisive share in breaking the aggressive spirit of the German Government and people.'

Untimely death and bereavement was undoubtedly the overriding experience of Portsmouth in the First World War, as it would be again twenty years later. To this burden of grief was added, in the immediate post-war period, the distress of unemployment, caused mainly by dockyard redundancies. It had been the same in 1815 and would be the

The Naval War Memorial in the early 1920s.

The Naval War Memorial today.

same again in 1945. Despite the Admiralty's reassurances in early 1918, these began in 1919, and were numerous and inevitable although the Admiralty did its best to mitigate the effect on the town by spreading them out, and by ordering the building of a 10,000-ton ship for commercial purposes although they never repeated this exercise. Relief schemes initiated in 1921 to provide work for the unemployed over the next few years included an extension of the esplanade past the Marine's Barracks at Eastney, the development of the Great Salterns, and the construction of two new roads, one from Portsbridge to the Southwick Road (to the west of High Street, Cosham) and another from Portsbridge across the marshes to the west of Wymering.

By the early 1920s, there were almost 7,000 unemployed. So serious was the distress in the town that the mayor re-opened the Goodwill Fund. This was a fund established in 1919 on the initiative of the *Evening News* to provide a Christmas dinner for men who had returned from the war and their families. The town had responded to the appeal with extraordinary generosity. The newspaper had hoped for £500. They raised £7,500 which more than paid for the dinner and allowed the organizers to administer relief to many distressed families during that winter. Once again, the response of the town to the new appeal for funds was remarkably generous. Some £6,000 was raised within a month and disbursed to 2,000 families. By the end of the year, £14,000 had been raised. The fund was not closed until April 1924.

The number of men of the Hampshire Regiment who died in action was published in 1920. They numbered 7,176 of which 1,375 served in the Portsmouth Battalions. To these figures must be added the Portsmouth men who died in service with other regiments, or who lost their lives at sea. Altogether it was a terrible toll. Had it been worth the sacrifice? Did Portsmouth change noticeably for the better after the war? Many of the widows and children struggled to survive, and many who came back safely returned to unemployment and hardship. John Leland's comments about Portsmouth almost 400 years before still rang true. The town was 'little occupied in time of pece[*sic*].' However the borough council was alert now to the vital need to try and diversify the local economy, and persuade the Admiralty and War Office to hand over land, surplus to their requirements, for development. Plans were also put in hand to address slum clearance and housing need, and these 'homes for heroes' were built during the following decade – their cottage-style architecture can be seen today throughout the city.

Whether it can be argued that social barriers were demonstrably breached during this war, as some commentators have suggested recently, is questionable in a town like Portsmouth, a naval port and garrison town, familiar with 'khaki' as Miss Kelly put it once, used to naval rank, privilege and discipline, and heavily dependent on naval work. Women were not strangers to the local workforce either, as they were in other parts of the country. The work they undertook during the war years was new, often heavy and demanding but they had been key players in the local economy for many years before the war. They deserved to be given the vote as much for their efforts historically as for their work now in the dockyard or on the trams. The returning troops and the enlarged electorate did not overturn the political *status quo* in Portsmouth in 1918. Conservatives were returned in Portsmouth North and Portsmouth South, and a Liberal in Portsmouth Central. In 1922, Conservatives were returned in all three seats and on the whole maintained their hold on power in the borough until the late twentieth century. In short, no new world order emerged in Portsmouth in the immediate post war years.

However what Portsmouth did prove, to itself and to others, during the First World War, was that it could mount a formidable volunteer effort as well as send its men away to fight. It is more usual to talk about the Second World War as the 'People's War' but many of Portsmouth's non-combatants fought a good fight, on their own doorsteps, during the First World War and, by so doing, made a significant contribution to the war effort.

The last word belongs to HMS *Centurion.* The ship spent an inglorious period between the wars being used as a gunnery target. By 1941, the superstructure and the hull sides were described in *Blackwood's Magazine* as looking like 'a much-travelled suitcase, a patchwork of rusty plates, a maze of rivets and welds'. Her subsequent career linked in a quite extraordinary way the events of the First World War and the settling of unfinished business which was the Second World War.

Early in 1941, HMS *Centurion* was put back into service. The boilers and engines were restored to working order, 'new' funnels and gun turrets were constructed – but this time from wood, steel and canvas – as painters and camouflage experts transformed the ship to replicate HMS *Anson,* then building in Portsmouth Dockyard, 'the pride of the Royal Navy' and 'Britain's latest sea-going monster'. With a skeleton crew on board, all useful gear, furniture and furnishings stripped out, and an ominous amount of explosives in the lower decks, the dummy *Anson* was destined to be sunk in Tripoli Harbour 'in another and more glorious' Zeebrugge. It would be a three-week cruise, the crew were promised, and they were to take minimum clothing and possessions with them. However, the plan was foiled because the naval force at Gibraltar which was to have escorted *Centurion* across the Mediterranean was diverted to search for the *Bismarck* which made an untimely appearance in the Atlantic.

Unescorted, the ship was sent south towards Freetown and like the legendary ghost ship, the *Flying Dutchman*, was not allowed to put into any of the usual ports of call such as Capetown and Durban. HMS *Centurion* continued round the Cape and finally dropped anchor three months, not three weeks, later, well out of the way, in the Great Bitter Lake in the Suez Canal. From there the ship was, in due course, despatched to Mombasa. From Aden, the vessel sailed into the south-west monsoon, which destroyed the dummy gun turrets and other pieces of superstructure as it manoeuvred with considerable difficulty through heavy seas. The old battleship was not up to the challenge though and returned to Aden before being moved, in due course, to Bombay. There a happy nine months was spent by the crew who, although they were anchored well offshore in the interests of security, made themselves at home by installing a piano, refrigerators, a wireless set and furniture on board. There was boating, bathing, cricket and football, and even dancing, when ashore.

In early 1942, their 'dummy' battleship was summoned back to Suez, to load supplies for the relief of Malta. The convoy was attacked though and HMS *Centurion* was hit. As the ship settled lower and lower in the water, it was decided to put back into Alexandria. When this port was evacuated by the Royal Navy the crew 'crabbed' their damaged ship back to Port Said, to block the Suez canal, if need be, but eventually finished up back on the Great Bitter Lake again, 'left like a dead thing'. That, thought the crew, was the last they would see

A panoramic view of part of the Mulberry harbour at the Arromanches beachhead. HMS Centurion *was sunk as a breakwater to protect the facilities.*

of the ship. However, early in 1944, those of them who were still in the Middle East were identified and, with others, formed into a new ship's company. HMS *Centurion* was taken to Alexandria where the enormous hole blown in the starboard side in 1942 was patched. Further repairs were carried out in Gibraltar and the ship arrived back finally in Devonport exactly three years to the day of sailing. From Devonport, HMS *Centurion* continued to Portsmouth.

Sailing up the English Channel, *Centurion* could still make 18kt and left the escort ships well behind. There was still life in the old ship. Manoeuvring up the Solent between lines of shipping 'awaiting the great Channel crossing', she entered Portsmouth Harbour, with the White Ensign and the Jolly Roger at the starboard yardarm. The 'great Channel crossing' was D-Day. Once again, the ship was stripped of all useful stores and equipment, and explosives were placed in the lower decks. The crew were advised, as before, to limit the amount of kit they took on board, and also that they would be back soon. This time they were. The ship was sent to Weymouth until required. On 7 June 1944, HMS *Centurion* was sunk off Arromanches on the Normandy coast to form part of the artificial breakwater of the Mulberry harbour, as described by the author of the article in *Blackwood's Magazine*:

'All around were hundreds of craft of all shapes and sizes. Five miles inland could be heard the roar of battle, though on the beaches it was comparatively quiet. Already the old ships had begun to be formed up into a breakwater, and as each was placed in position there was a cloud of smoke, followed by a dull boom as the scuttling charges went off and the ships slowly settled.

We steamed into position, aided by two tugs. Down in the engine-room the last few movements of the throttles were made. Then came the order, "Finished with main engines for ever!" Followed by the

order, "Everyone on deck." There was a brief pause, and then the captain gave the order, "Fire charges."'

HMS *Centurion* gave a convulsive leap, there was a cloud of dust which belched out of all the funnels and ventilators, and the great ship began to sink. When the ship came to rest on the bottom it was no longer a ship – a dreadnought. It was now a breakwater. The crew then abandoned ship. Reportedly, the Germans thought the old ship had been sunk by shore batteries with great loss of life as they saw only seventy men leaving the sinking ship. This was in fact the whole ship's company.

We met this ship at Jutland, thirty years before. HMS *Centurion* had been launched in 1911 by Clementine Churchill, the wife of Winston Churchill who was now, in 1944, Prime Minister. Then he was First Lord of the Admiralty. HMS *Centurion* lay now off the coast of France a derelict hulk but, in the words of *Blackwood's Magazine,* the ship had played a part, this time at the finish, 'in putting Europe to rights'. It is a fitting tribute 100 years after the outbreak of the First World War and in the 70th anniversary year of D-Day.

Bibliography

There are no footnotes in this book. I hope I have made my sources obvious in the text. If not they should be clear in the list below.

Ashworth, G.J., *Portsmouth's Political Patterns 1885-1945*, Portsmouth Paper (PP) No.24, 1976.

Blackwoods Magazine, January 1946.

Eley, Philip, *Portsmouth Breweries 1492-1847*, PP. No.51, 1988.

Eley, Philip, *Portsmouth Breweries since 1947*, PP. No.63, 1994.

Eley, Philip and Riley, R.C., *The Demise of Demon Drink? Portsmouth Pubs 1900-1950,* PP. No.58, 1991.

Gates, W.G. (Ed), *Portsmouth and the Great War*, Portsmouth, 1919.

Gates, W.G. and successors (Eds), *Records of the Corporation, 1835-1974*, 7 vols. Portsmouth, 1928-83.

Gladstone, F.C., *The Memoirs of Frederick Charles Gladstone 1889-1966*, 2006.

Gossop, Nigel, *Tales of Pluck and Daring. The Life and Work of Percy F. Westerman*, Portsmouth Grammar School (PGS) Monograph No.24.

Gough, Paul, *A Terrible Beauty: British Artists in the First World War*, 2010.

Lunn, Ken and Day, Ann (Eds), *Inside the Wall. Recollections of*

Portsmouth Dockyard, 1900-1950, University of Portsmouth, 1998.

National Museum of the Royal Navy (NMRN)

The diaries and letters of the following:

Commander Arthur Layard, NMRN 1990.271

Rear Admiral Reginald Tupper, NMRN 187.130

Lieutenant James Colvill, NMRN 1997.43

Lieutenant Commander Donald MacGregor, NMRN 1990.192

Stoker Albert Farley, NMRN 1990.150

Lieutenant George Lloyd, NMRN 2004.23

Leading Seaman David Bain, NMRN 1992.126

Chief Petty Officer A.W. Young, NMRN 1992.1997

Unnamed Rating on HMS *Implacable* at Gallipoli, NMRN 2000.82

Commander Knightley Boase, NMRN 1991.89

Lieutenant L.G.P. Vereker, NMRN 2003.42

Master at Arms Herbert Simkins, NMRN. 2000.81

Able Seaman Gunner Frank Greenwood, NMRN 2003.9

Chief Petty Officer Edwin Fletcher, NMRN 1980.15

Peacock, Sarah, *Borough Government in Portsmouth, 1835-1974'*, PP. No.23, 1975.

Peacock, Sarah, *Votes for Women: The Women's Fight for the Vote in Portsmouth*, PP No.39, 1983.

Portsmouth History Centre, Central Library, Guildhall Square:

The Portsmouth Times, 1914-19

The Evening News, 1914-18

Portsmouth Borough Council and Committee Minutes, 1914-19

St Mary's Portsea Parish Magazines, 1914-19

Medical Officer of Health Reports, 1914-19

1911 Census Reports for Portsmouth

Records of the Milton Home Industry for War Widows, *c.*1916 to *c.*1939, 471A.

Correspondence of Lieutenant R.C. Rundell, Hampshire Regiment, 1915-17, 1002A.

Quail, Sarah, Barrett, George and Chessun, Christopher (Eds), *Consecrated to Prayer. A Centenary History of St Mary's, Portsea 1889-1989,* 1989.

Quail, Sarah, *The Origins of Portsmouth and the First Charter*, PP. No.65, 1994.

Quail, Sarah and Wilkinson, Alan (Eds), *Forever Building: Essays to Mark the Completion of the Cathedral Church of St Thomas of Canterbury Portsmouth,* 1995.

Quail, Sarah, *Southsea Past,* 2000.

Sadden, John, *Portsmouth and Gosport at War,* 2012.

Stedman, John (Ed.), *People of Portsmouth: The 20th Century in Their Own Words*, 2002.

Stevens, F.E, *The Battle Story of the Hampshire Regiment, 1709-1919.*

Webb, John, Quail, Sarah, Haskell, Patricia and Riley, Ray, *The Spirit of Portsmouth. A History,* 1989.

Webb, John, *The City of Portsmouth College of Education 1907-1976,* PGS Monograph Series No.23.

Index